How Millennials Can Lead Us Out of the Mess We're In

How Millennials Can Lead Us Out of the Mess We're In

A Jew, a Muslim, and a Christian Share Leadership Lessons from the Life of Moses

MORDECAI SCHREIBER,
IQBAL UNUS, AND
IAN CASE PUNNETT

ROWMAN & LITTLEFIELD
Lanham • Boulder • New York • London

Published by Rowman & Littlefield
An imprint of The Rowman & Littlefield Publishing Group, Inc.
4501 Forbes Boulevard, Suite 200, Lanham, Maryland 20706
www.rowman.com

6 Tinworth Street, London SE11 5AL, United Kingdom

Distributed by NATIONAL BOOK NETWORK

British Library Cataloguing in Publication Information Available

Library of Congress Cataloging-in-Publication Data

Names: Schreiber, Mordecai, author. | Unus, Iqbal J., author. | Punnett, Ian, 1960– author.
Title: How Millennials can lead us out of the mess we're in : a Jew, a Muslim, and a Christian share leadership lessons from the life of Moses / Mordecai Schreiber, Iqbal Unus, and Ian Case Punnett.
Description: Lanham : Rowman & Littlefield, [2020] | Includes index. | Summary: "'How Millennials Can Lead Us Out of the Mess We're In' brings together an Israeli-born rabbi, a Pakistani-born Muslim scholar, and an ordained Midwestern American to inspire the next generation of leaders with a timeless story of the ancient prophet Moses"— Provided by publisher.
Identifiers: LCCN 2019057081 (print) | LCCN 2019057082 (ebook) | ISBN 9781538134108 (cloth) | ISBN 9781538134115 (epub)
Subjects: LCSH: Moses (Biblical leader) | Moses (Biblical leader)—Islamic interpretations. | Leadership—Religious aspects. | Leadership—Biblical teaching. | Leadership.
Classification: LCC BS580.M6 S357 2020 (print) | LCC BS580.M6 (ebook) | DDC 222/.1092—dc23
LC record available at https://lccn.loc.gov/2019057081
LC ebook record available at https://lccn.loc.gov/2019057082

To my colleagues, Ian Punnett and Iqbal Unus, for the great honor of working with them on this trailblazing book, and whose friendship I cherish.

—*Rabbi Mordecai Schreiber*

To the children of my favorite mixed marriage, Anne Florence Bartosch and James Joseph Bartosch. I regret that my commitments prevented me from standing with you during your respective religious ceremonies welcoming you into adulthood. I would have loved to have been a conversation partner with you as you grew in your parents' traditions. May this book succeed where I have failed.

—*Reverend Ian Case Punnett, PhD*

To the leadership in all of us.

—*Dr. Iqbal Unus*

Contents

Preface

No Jew can speak for all Jews; no Christian can speak for all Christians; no Muslim can speak for all Muslims. Our three faiths lack a unified voice. We all march to the sound of different drummers.

Those drums become cacophonous, though, when the three faiths interface because, historically, we are rarely on the same beat. We have been at war with one another for centuries, and in many places in the world today, we still are. Sometimes we call each other names; sometimes name-calling leads to people-killing. There have been very few years without war somewhere in our mutual history.

Can we put an end to a seemingly endless cycle of hatred and violence? And if so, where do we begin?

One Jew, one Christian, and one Muslim believe it all begins with leadership. Many world leaders today have grown entitled and lazy. Too often, our collective futures are in the hands of demagogues who use toxic weapons of hatred and fear to gain power and keep it. Some leaders start with the good of their people at heart, but luxury and flattery warp the good that is within until they become heirs to history's worst despots and tyrants.

Time could be running out on our small, fragile, overpopulated planet. If we are living on a powder keg, then fanning the sparks of suspicion and prejudice will never end well. The time to act was a million yesterdays ago, but we lack a time machine. Those of us living today can only take responsibility for future yesterdays. Otherwise, we court our peril.

If we speak as mere individuals, we risk our voices being drowned out by the perpetual yawn of the cynical status quo. But one Jew, one Christian, and one Muslim speaking as one voice could thunder like millions yelling into a canyon. It is possible to be singing from the same hymnal if we just focus on our common beliefs.

This one Jew, this one Christian, and this one Muslim believe there is only one human race, that God is one, that the same God inspires us all, and that we share a destiny. Our common enemy is not each other, but rather those who decry that there is nothing divine about Creation, nothing sacred worth honoring, and that we should worship riches, power, sex, or human celebrities that serve as idols.

We also believe that we have a choice on how we treat each other and that the past does not have to be prologue. As Jews, Christians, and Muslims, we are all spiritual descendants of Abraham and disciples of Moses. Abraham was a man of peace, and Moses was a liberator and lawgiver who found the path to the Promised Land. If we let him, Moses—our common role model of leadership—will guide us to fulfill the prophecy of Isaiah: "Nation shall not raise a sword against another nation, nor shall they learn war anymore."

Honoring the story of Moses does not mean we are forced to tell the story only one way or only allowed to learn one lesson. In this book, one Jew, one Christian, and one Muslim have joined their hands together to hold one pen, and though we may write from different minds, it is from the same heart.

May the Almighty illumine our eyes and show us the path to a new Promised Land where we all can live as brothers and sisters.

Amen.

Introduction

The World Needs Many Moseses

Times of great flux require people with strong, innovative leadership skills to move forward toward a new stability. In the United States, for example, many Americans have experienced some level of chaos from the top down since the election of President Donald Trump. Countries that were once our allies have been treated as enemies, and notoriously evil dictators have been lauded as misunderstood friends and even called "great." The rise in anti-immigrant hostility—much of it directed toward Muslims, Mexicans, and Latin American asylum seekers—has resulted in the deaths of innocent people. Conversely, a resurgence in white supremacy movements has been condemned only infrequently from the White House and sometimes excused as the bad actions of "good people."

In other news from "the upside down," Evangelical Christians—once predictable critics of even borderline immoral behavior of public figures—endorsed Trump and provided reliable cover for his past, unbounded sexual appetites that resulted in serial divorces and marriages. Inexplicable to many people of faith, polls indicate that the Christian Right has proudly produced what amounts to an endless stack of "get out of moral jail free" cards for Trump and his associates. While the epicenter for these shaky times in the United States appears to be the Oval Office, global aftershocks have had similar destabilizing effects in every corner of the world.

Benjamin Franklin's proposed Great Seal of the United States featured Moses parting the Red Sea, Pharaoh's army drowning, and rays of fire extending to the sky that symbolized the power of God imparting justice. John Adams and Thomas Jefferson were also part of the first committee to design a Great Seal for this new nation. No consensus was reached with Franklin, and future designs for our Great Seal went in a different direction. Something about a bird. (Image courtesy of Wikimedia Commons, https://commons.wikimedia.org/wiki/File:FirstCommitteeGreatSealReverseLossingDrawing.jpg)

By all appearances, the whole world is in a polarizing period caught between a younger generation that prefers peace and collaboration, and demands its voice be heard, on one end, and aging autocratic leaders and old-fashioned tyrants who attempt to keep power centralized to themselves, on the other. There is no disputing that, according to the 2016 US

Electoral College, many American voters preferred the "my primary consultant is myself," go-it-alone, authoritarian leadership style of President Donald J. Trump—at least for a while. The president has millions of fans and defenders, and probably always will, but as Dr. Jean Twenge observes in *Psychology Today*, typically, those Americans are not Millennial voters who were born between the early 1980s and the mid-1990s. Not much research is in yet about Gen Z young adults—the generation of highly educated workers coming behind Millennials—but according to early indications from Pew Research Center, about half of self-identifying Gen Z Republicans mirror typical Millennial liberal social views.

From the beginning, Millennials, the largest generation to ever enter the American workforce thus far, were much more likely to be against Trump's style of leadership than for it. Some segments of the Millennial bloc did come out in support of President Trump on election day, mainly young whites, but according to Pew's study in March 2018, "Millennial voters continue to have the highest proportion of independents of any generation. But when their partisan leanings are taken into account, they also are the most Democratic generation." Regardless of whether they voted for him, based on Pew's surveys conducted over the first couple years of Trump's presidency, about two-thirds of Millennial voters currently disapprove of how President Trump is running the country. Midway through the next decade, Millennials will account for more than 50 percent of all American employees.

Based on characteristics of the Millennial generation, this disconnect could have been anticipated. While anecdotal research suggests that Millennials deeply resent being stereotyped with overly broad descriptors, empirical research indicates that Millennials across the country have much in common. Millennials are idealists; they prefer collaboration to zero-sum competition. Millennials like to be successful, but, contrary to the generation that is passing, winning at all costs is discouraged—and certainly not at the cost of one's soul.

Millennial values appear to be baked in. For example, this generation doesn't have to "embrace diversity" because, to them, diversity is second nature. They value differences in each other and are mindful of the experience that everybody else is having. Millennials do well under strong leadership, but only if they look up to that person. Leaders of Millennials—of any age or background—must be fair, have integrity, and be concerned more about people and the world than the bottom line to earn their respect. For these reasons and more, Millennials in the workplace can present unique challenges to "top-down, authoritarian" management styles of autocrats and tyrants.

Trump's election by Americans who yearned for an authoritarian, power-centralized version of democracy appears to be the result of years of frustration with past national leaders. Trump's campaign pledge that "I alone can fix it" may have seemed plausible to older voters given the reality television star's appearance of business success. Millennials take a dimmer view of that posturing, however. For example, Trump boasts that, when it comes to important foreign policy decisions, he confers primarily with himself "because I have a very good brain, and I've said a lot of things." Such is not the Millennial way. Neither are his demands to lock up his political rivals, his attempts to brand the free press as "an enemy of the people," or his frequent hints that he would like to be president for life. These are the stylings of a tyrant.

But Millennials are not the only group to push back against such an approach. As of this publication, a majority of Gen Xers disapprove of how Trump is managing the country, and Baby Boomers are roughly around fifty-fifty. As of this printing, only the oldest Americans over-whelmingly support the president's handling of domestic and foreign issues, and that group is getting smaller every year. As the "Greatest Generation" passes on and Millennials and Gen Xers age up, the world is watching the United States transition from a nation of "life as we know it" to a nation of "what's next?" With Millennials taking over power positions, Donald Trump's autocratic style may be the last of its kind for a while.

Either way, whether one wishes for it or not, change is as inevitable as calamity; the only control humanity has over the outcome is in how well it is prepared to meet both. As director James Cameron once said about the current zeitgeist, "We're living in the time *between* when the look-out saw the iceberg, and when the *Titanic* hit the iceberg." Avoiding and/or grappling with disaster will require not just the best leadership but also new, creative thinking at every level in society to manage "what's next." If the past is prologue, times of great flux will require great leadership to shepherd communities to Promised Lands of peace and prosperity that wait on the other side of doubt and fear. Regardless of political persuasion, many people have forgotten what great leadership even looks like.

One of history's earliest examples of a leader with both a strong vision and a concern for the welfare of others—the classic Millennial model— is still the best example: the prophet Moses. A thirteenth-century BCE "super shepherd," Moses was a Jew who was born in Egyptian captivity, rose to prominence in Pharaoh's court, and then spent years in contemplative exile before freeing his people from slavery and delivering the foundation for much of our modern law.

In the story that is told in the Bible and the Qur'an, Moses exemplifies resistance to cruel authority through his continued personal development as an effective leader. Moses ("Moshe" in Hebrew; "Musa" as his name is rendered in Arabic) appears in four of the first five books of the Bible while a similar narrative of Moses is the longest and most detailed story of all the prophets told in Islam's most holy book, the Qur'an.

Because of Moses' legendary resistance to tyrannical oppression, Benjamin Franklin's first proposed Great Seal of the United States featured an image of Moses parting the Red Sea, Pharaoh's army drowning, and rays of God's dazzling power in the sky. Surrounding the composite image was Franklin's proposed motto for the fledgling United States: "Rebellion to tyrants is Obedience to God." It never caught on. Fair's fair; it is a little heavy-handed. How many countries have a national seal centered on an image of an about-to-be-dead tyrant and his followers?

For those wanting to be the best possible leader to a goal-oriented generation of greater-good-focused Millennials, Franklin's interest in a Mosaic model of leadership still instructs. For the non-religious, simply

Stories about the specialness of the relationship between God and the Hebrew tribes are collected in an elaborate covenant (that is, an agreement) between God and Jews known as the Torah (also sometimes called by its Greek name, Pentateuch). The Torah comprises the first five books of the larger Hebrew Bible—so, many books within a book—usually referred to by their individual, Westernized titles: Genesis, Exodus, Leviticus, Numbers, and Deuteronomy. These are also known as "the Five Books of Moses" because they contain the Moses story from beginning to end.

The Hebrew Bible is almost exactly the same as the first section of the even longer Christian Bible, which categorizes the Hebrew Bible as the Old Testament. The New Testament contains only Christian-focused writings that were collected in the first centuries after the birth of Jesus. The Holy Bible (as most Christians know it) was not codified completely until the fifth century. Up until that point, various versions, which included some parts but not others, had been shared for hundreds of years. Hearing a reference to the Bible, Jews would likely be inclined to think only of the part before the New Testament, while Christians would think of both.

The special relationship between Israel and God, however, is also recorded in the Qur'an, which was written a thousand years after the Hebrew Bible appeared and centuries after the Christian Bible began the process of codification. Like the Christian Bible, but unlike the Hebrew Bible, the Qur'an also features stories of John the Baptist and Jesus of Nazareth and his disciples. In fact, Moses and Jesus are just two of the approximately fifty biblical characters shared by Christians and Muslims (and almost as many by Muslims and Jews).

swap the word "good" for "God." "Rebellion to tyrants is Obedience to Good" still works as a motto in a political crisis, certain family situations, neighborhood conflict, or standing up to a bullying boss. Whereas even "rebellion" may sound too violent or confrontational, "resistance" evokes the same spirit. "Resistance to tyrants is Obedience to Good" is just as valid a guiding ethos as Franklin's summation of the Moses story.

According to the biblical and qur'anic texts, however, for Jews, Christians, and Muslims, it is the humble style of Moses' servant leadership that teaches the reader the most. Pharaoh's demise came despite Moses' best efforts to show him a better way than human exploitation and cruelty. Accordingly, this book (a collaboration between an Israeli-born American rabbi, a Washington, D.C.–area Muslim scholar who came from what is now modern-day Pakistan, and a seminary-trained American Christian professor at Kansas State University) is focused on how Moses' confident, competent humility ultimately led to his success against nearly impossible odds—and how that ancient story can still inform our modern approach to problem solving.

Nobody is suggesting there is any "profit" in imitating Moses, but, to borrow a phrase from the culinary arts, tomorrow's leaders would benefit from being more "Moses forward." Being "Moses forward" means understanding, prioritizing, and, finally, incorporating a Mosaic style of leadership into our relationships with those who are in power in our lives by taking a "deep dive" into the controversial decisions by the greatest leader of all time. This book will both fill in the blanks for those only passingly familiar with the Moses narrative and challenge people of all faiths to reconsider what they thought they learned in Sunday School. Good people—whether they practice a faith or observe no religious tradition at all—can resist the resurgence in global authoritarianism by focusing on our shared spiritual heritage.

All readers are the future leaders for which the world is waiting. There is plenty of work to be done in every corner of global society. In business, in not-for-profit work, in charity, in community organizing,

the future will go to those who understand that a period of great reconciliation and providence is possible by new leaders who will put people
over politics. A study of Moses could improve best practices in every
type of organization.

So, whether your ear is tuned to the blow of a shofar, the adhan from
a muezzin, the clang of a distant church belfry, a referee's whistle, or the
opening and closing bell of Wall Street, if you are a leader of any age,
gender, or religion (or no religion at all), or if you are aspiring to be the
leader you feel you are inside, the world has opportunities for a few good
Moseses, and this book could be your "burning bush."

1

A Quick Refresher Course on Moses

Many are the Moseses in our lives. Representations of Moses in our religious traditions vary to some degree. Although the Jewish and Christian images of Moses are very similar, it would be fair to say that Moses' "Jewishness" is emphasized in traditional Jewish imagery while a "Christian" version of Moses might appear more European. Elsewhere, in Steven Spielberg's animated *Prince of Egypt* (1998), Moses appears distinctly Middle Eastern, and Ridley Scott's violent, atheistic, Eurocentric *Exodus: Gods and Kings* (2014) is so un-Jewish it starred an actor named Christian Bale.

Cecil B. DeMille made two versions of the Moses story, first as a young director in the silent movie era and then his later widescreen Technicolor version of *The Ten Commandments* (1923; 1956), both of which were proud products of his Episcopal Church upbringing. In fact, DeMille cast fellow Episcopalian Charlton Heston as Moses in the latter film, arguably the most famous cinematic image of Moses. Because of the repeat TV showings of *The Ten Commandments* (1956) around the world—a movie that was billed as a depiction of "the birth of freedom"—if the average person has a mental picture of Moses, it is of Heston in a series of glued-on beards and leather wrist straps holding a staff with his arms raised toward heaven.

The qur'anic Moses narrative largely parallels the Bible with some key differences. According to Hollywood historians, the screenwriters for *The Ten Commandments* (1956) pulled on every available ancient source regarding Moses, including the Qur'an, but it is anybody's guess how many Muslims have ever seen the movie. The making or displaying images or statues of religious figures is strictly prohibited in Islam, but that does not mean they have not happened at all. Persia—modern-day Iran—had completely converted to Islam by the eleventh century CE; yet a fifteenth-century Persian painting of Moses with Abraham, Jesus, and Muhammed proves that art images of qur'anic figures were popular as illustrations in books. Technically, even a Hollywood movie such as *The Ten Commandments*, made by non-Muslims, violates the dictum that non-prohibited acts (such as moviemaking) which lead to prohibited acts (e.g., personifying prophets or messengers of God and taking creative liberties with their life stories) are to be avoided.

In popular, non-religious media, there is also a "public" Moses that appears as an ethnically neutral "Sunday School" version typically found in instructive stories for children. In various animated *VeggieTales* versions of Exodus, for example, Moses is either a zucchini or a cucumber, or perhaps a pickle—one of those; it's hard to tell. Typical of children's versions of the Moses narrative, in the *VeggieTales* series, the deaths of Egyptian children are played down and phrased vaguely. Each of these cinematic Moseses centers around overlapping but sometimes competing narratives intended to communicate lessons at various stages of our lives, but the overall effect is a general public that is left with contrasting, overly broad impressions of who Moses was.

This is why people who think they understand Moses because they have watched Charlton Heston in widescreen Technicolor, Christian Bale's "Dark Knight" Moses, or the PG-rated *Prince of Egypt* are still missing the complexity of the authentic Moses. For example, according to urban legend, Heston was chosen to play Moses by DeMille because DeMille thought Heston resembled Michelangelo's *Moses*, a sixteenth-century carving for the tomb of Pope Julius II.

Because the main goal of this book is to discuss how the life story of Moses as understood by three great faiths can invigorate the servant leadership the world needs today, background on the religious texts that bring the Moses narrative to life is required from time to time in the pages ahead. The Hebrew Bible, the Holy Bible per Christianity, and the Qur'an form the nexus of this book's discussion.

In addition, a companion book of commentary on the Qur'an, the Hadith, plays an important role. The Qur'an and Hadith lay out the indisputable framework expected of Muslims to perform their duties to God and humankind. For Muslims, no other texts merit attention and obedience. That said, the fourteenth-century Muslim commentary titled *Stories of the Prophets* by renowned qur'anic scholar Ibn Kathir—who today would be considered an imam, or teacher—also plays an important part because of his colorful insight into the qur'anic texts. For Muslims worldwide, *Stories of the Prophets* can be considered an accepted text that contains much of the Moses story, even though it is largely a topical Hadith collection with some reference to biblical works. The reader should be mindful that the Qur'an itself and Ibn Kathir's version of the qur'anic stories may be used interchangeably to advance the Moses narrative for the purposes of this book, but they are not the same.

Finally, in the Muslim tradition, when the name of Muhammed or any prophet or messenger in Islam is mentioned, the phrase "Peace be upon him" is attached. When writing in English, the acrostic "PBUH" is an acceptable abbreviation. The Muslim or even non-Muslim reader is encouraged to remember this addition and insert it when applicable.

Both the Bible and the Qur'an accentuate that Moses had a speech impediment of some kind about which he was self-conscious; yet the "movie Moseses" that the public knows so well rarely reflect any sign of a stutter, a lisp, a damaged palate, or any evidence of what the Bible stipulates was a man "heavy of mouth and heavy of tongue." Whereas Jewish, Christian, and Islamic scholars have debated the true nature of Moses' affliction and what it implies about the text, Hollywood eliminates this valuable characteristic by giving Moses enviable oratorical skills and a booming God-like voice.

Some commentary in the Hadith, the second-highest-ranking book in Islam after the Qur'an, even suggests that Moses was actually a black African—or at least very dark brown skinned—with black curly hair.

The Hadith is a companion book to the Qur'an. Meaning, roughly, "speech," "report," or "narrative" in Arabic, the Hadith is a collection of things that the Prophet Muhammed said during his lifetime that were recorded by his acolytes and later collected into a book. Just as not all Jews would consider the New Testament as legitimate as the Hebrew Bible, not all Muslims accept the Hadith—or at least all of it—as "divine revelation." Nonetheless, for most Muslims, the Hadith contains significant material regarding Islamic religious law and moral teaching.

As a point of national pride, Ethiopians of various religious backgrounds have insisted that Moses came from Ethiopia. In sum, the creative decisions needed to drive a successful box office in America have left their mark on the "public Moses" and obscured the truth of the text in the process.

Popularized distortions of holy texts that are manipulated to create an easily followed narrative for a mass audience attest to Islam's prohibition on the making of images of the prophets. Both the public "*Braveheart* Moses" in Scott's *Exodus* and the "Cecil B. DeMoses" of *The Ten Commandments* tell the Moses story without the nuance, subtlety, and ambiguity of the biblical or qur'anic accounts. This was the director's intention; DeMille maintained that bringing Bible stories to non-Bible readers was his ministry.

Some argue there never was a "real" Moses at all, just a mythic leader with no historical foundation, a stance that would reduce all understandings of Moses to be as "imaginary" as a *VeggieTales* "Cucumber Moses" asking "Yamses II" to "Let my pickles go"—or was that in *The Simpsons*? Anyway, according to some Bible scholars, Moses is simply a composite figure of several leaders who had evolved over time to codify and transmit the history and laws of Judaism.

Which is why, again, for the purposes of this discussion, one does not have to have faith in any kind of Creator-God. It is possible for a person of no faith to invest in a Moses narrative as merely an allegorical tale of clashing forces that expects humans to confront evil whenever it threatens the good. This is to say, if the Moses narrative is too big for any one religious tradition, as the many "public Moseses" indicated, it has already been proven to be too powerful to be confined to religion at all. Ultimately, it is a simple story of an inspired person who challenged injustice and cruelty and led the oppressed to freedom—perhaps with nothing more than the belief that things can get better and the sheer determination to be the change agent that is going to make it happen.

For millions of Jews, Christians, and Muslims, Moses represents humanity at its best and the belief that anybody can perform miracles if they walk with God. This was certainly the case of the Moses story as it was told in the Bible, but it was a walk that started generations before him. Judaism, Christianity, and Islam are also connected through Abraham, another common patriarch, which is why they are referred to as the "Three Great Abrahamic Religions." In the book of Genesis, God promised Abraham (originally named "Abram" at birth), "I will make you into a great nation, and I will bless you; I will make your name great, and you will be a blessing." Similarly, in chapter 2 of the Qur'an, God said to Abraham, "Behold, I shall make thee a leader of men," although not in the political sense. The Qur'an speaks of Abraham as an *imam* (Arabic for "moral guide"), perhaps due to the many virtuous qualities that Abraham displayed when he discouraged his people from worshiping idols, his total obedience to God, and his unconditional trust in a divine plan. So, although Abraham—the father of Jews and Arabs—was an exemplary human being whose admirable qualities included humility, hospitality, and great faith, he was not a leader in the purest sense because neither the Bible nor the Qur'an speaks of Abraham as having an opportunity to lead a group of unrelated followers to accomplish a specific, history-changing goal. For that honor, God chose Moses— peace be upon him.

For those unfamiliar with either the Bible or the Qur'an, the back-story in the Moses narrative begins with a righteous man named Jacob, the grandson of Abraham and later the father of twelve sons by two wives and two concubines (a marital companion that is not a slave but also not a wife). In the Qur'an, Jacob is identified as an important and pious prophet, but his narrative lacks the details of the Bible. Just as God had changed Abram's original name to Abraham to mark the prophet's growing stature, in Genesis 32, after a night when Jacob wrestled with an angel either literally or in a dreamlike state, Jacob is told that as a continuing sign that God has given the man a divine blessing, Jacob would live out his days with a new name: "Israel."

For such an important event in history, oddly, the exact meaning of Israel has been lost over time, but consensus scholarship suggests some variation of a Hebrew phrase meaning "struggles with God." His descendants are termed "Israelites." Israel's twelve sons and their growing families, the "Twelve Tribes of Israel" (as they have come to be known), became the foundation of the unified Hebrew nation of the same name.

The phrase "Children of Israel," therefore, has both a literal and a meta-phorical context in references to Jews today.

Concurrent with much of this narrative, Joseph—Israel's eleventh son but the first with his most beloved and final wife, Rachel—was in Egypt after having been tricked by his jealous brothers and sold into slavery. Because of his God-given ability to prophesy (meaning to pass along divine messages about potential future outcomes), however, Joseph ultimately prospered and saved Egypt, the nation to the southwest where he rose to become a benevolent vizier, which is a kind of prime minister in the court of the Egyptian Pharaoh. It was during this period that the man who had been renamed Israel, his eleven other sons, and all their families were reunited with Joseph after a famine in their homeland sent them searching for food. After Joseph forgave his brothers for selling him into slavery, Israel's entire extended clan migrated to live in Egypt and remained there under royal aegis for generations.

Because the descendants of Israel were non-national Egyptians who maintained their own Jewish customs in relative isolation as their community grew, as time passed, the Twelve Tribes of Israel became perceived as an "other" to the "real" Egyptians. Eventually, an unnamed pharaoh of an unspecified time before Moses became fearful that although the Hebrews were still a minority, their growing population constituted an internal threat to his reign if they were to align themselves with Egypt's external enemies. This situation led to fear, persecution, and, finally, enslavement by an Egyptian majority who worked the Israelites to death in the building of a Pharaonic empire. By the time of Moses, in an effort to curb the "threat" of a half million Jews, a pharaoh whom neither the Qur'an nor the Bible names had ordered all newborn male children of the Israelites to be murdered. Although movies such as *The Ten Commandments* identify this pharaoh as Ramses II, there is no scriptural or historical evidence to support this contention. However, regardless of who he was, the purge was on.

To avoid the massacre of male Hebrew babies by Pharaoh, after the child who would become Moses was three months old, Jochebed, Moses' birth mother, put him in a papyrus cradle that was coated in waterproof tar and pitch and floated him on the Nile in hopes that the baby would survive miraculously. Because Moses' brother Aaron (Harun, in Arabic) was already around three years old, he was not subject to the edict of infanticide and was safe. The boys' older sister, Miriam (the specific name of Moses' sister is not given in the Qur'an), watched in secret from the reedy shore as the child drifted out into the river current.

Exodus Tales of Prophet Moosa and Prophet Haroon by Muhammad Vandestra is another informative source. The Qur'an indicates that a woman from Pharaoh's household, possibly his wife (also unnamed), plucked the newborn from his hastily made baby boat and brought him to the palace, where Pharaoh's wife raised him as her own because, as Ibn Kathir phrased it, Pharaoh "was a disbeliever; she was a believer. He was cruel; she was merciful. He was a tyrant; she was delicate and good-hearted." For Pharaoh's wife, this child was an answer to a sad prayer "because she was infertile and had hoped to have a son. Hardly had she held the baby than she kissed him."

In a version of the story told in Jewish lore, the baby's Hebrew name was Chaver; it was Pharaoh's *daughter* who spotted the floating crib in the Nile, and it was she who gave him the Egyptian name Moses, meaning, presumably, "one taken out" in ancient Egyptian because he had been taken out of the river. A quick-thinking Miriam, who had followed Moses' rescue from the banks, then emerged from hiding to convince the palace to employ Moses' actual, grieving mother to be his wet nurse and help raise the boy. In some versions, baby Moses rejected all wet nurses until a national search led them back to Jochebed. What blessed one was now blessing all.

As a result, according to Judaism, Moses knew that he was adopted from the Hebrews. As he got older, Moses married a beautiful palace visitor from the land of Kush, a region roughly equivalent to modern-day Ethiopia. (Many Ethiopian scholars cite Moses' introduction to a Kushite woman as proof that Moses himself was at least partially Ethiopian.) Later, Moses' curiosity compelled him to leave the royal confines to observe and interact with his own people, where he witnessed the suffering of the Hebrew slaves firsthand. Later, in an act of spontaneous rage, when Moses saw an Egyptian overseer (who was likely a Jew himself) mistreating a Hebrew worker, Moses fought with the abusive taskmaster and killed him, entirely by accident, according to the Qur'an; the Bible is not so generous on that point: "Looking this way and that and seeing no one, he killed the Egyptian and hid him in the sand."

All three traditions agree that somehow Pharaoh learned of the overseer's killing and put out a death warrant on Moses. Fearing retribution from their rulers, the Hebrew slaves joined with the Egyptians in condemning Moses, which forced Moses to flee his Kushite wife and wander the desert until he came to a community near the Red Sea in the northwestern part of the Arab peninsula controlled by the tribes of Midian, descendants of Abraham through Keturah, his second wife. Although the Midianites no longer worshiped the God of Abraham, a successful shepherd named Jethro, a direct descendant of Abraham and a Midianite priest who (according to the Qur'an, at least) was still true to his Hebrew roots, learned of Moses from his daughters, who had met him drawing water at their well. Jethro took pity on the traveler and employed him as a shepherd. Jethro soon saw greatness in Moses and married him to a daughter. It was as a humble shepherd, an ordinary person, that God first spoke to Moses directly and elevated him to the status of prophet, a human who speaks for God.

While it is true that God had been preparing Moses from childhood to adulthood to become a prophet, Moses was still a mere mortal prone to human mistakes. God did not give up on Moses, and Moses did not give up on God. Moses had been spared the undertow of the Nile, retribution for the death of the cruel overseer, and the treacheries of banishment, but, on paper at least, the length of Moses' life was more about divine protection than a result of any consistent display of leadership skills.

In the chapters ahead, after a discussion of the most modern leadership styles and management models that the Mosaic style still addresses,

There are several types of messengers of God in scripture. For most of the Bible, angels are spirit beings who appear so human that the people they encounter do not notice. Angels have personalities, they seem to have their own wills, and they can make choices. Angels never were human beings; human beings can never be angels. When they act as God's representative, it is rarely good news. Also, angels can be used as God's stand-ins, so to speak, as it often happens that one second an angel is speaking and the next moment God is present.

Prophets and prophetesses are human men and women who have been given the ability to speak *for* God—that is, their mouths repeat God's words perfectly. Prophets usually reflect God's optimism that, given alternatives, human beings will choose the right path. Moses becomes an eternal bond between creation and its Creator, and Moses is the most revered of all the Hebrew prophets.

Islamic culture absorbed a pre-Muslim concept of the *jinn*—unseen, supernatural beings that, like angels, have free will to make good and bad decisions. The jinn—or, as the word comes to us in English, genies—play a kind of "devil's advocate" role in tandem with angels.

the answer to this central question—"Why exactly did God turn a fugitive, overprivileged palace dweller into a great leader for the ages?"—will explain why, in the eyes of God, anybody could serve as the next Moses. The story of Moses' breakthrough leadership will demonstrate how, if nothing else, deliverance from chaos starts with a triumph of imagination over cynicism. It was not just human imagination that was needed to resolve the crisis of leadership that had brought about the enslavement of a generation of Jews under Pharaoh but also divine imagination. In picking Moses, God was thinking out of the box, too.

Whether for you he was Moshe, Musa, or Moses—regardless of whether you think of him as Hebrew, Ethiopian, or a cartoon pickle in kid's movie—the Mosaic story still informs any discussion of leadership in times of tyrants. The shared blueprint of the biblical and qur'anic texts has provided guidance to many over the centuries, but, to that list, let us add this age in which a new class of cruelty is dominating the world stage. At a time when Fox News' Tucker Carlson can refuse to defend Kim Jong-un for murdering his political rivals and his own innocent citizens and then go on to defend him in the very next breath by saying, "You've got to be honest about what it means to lead a country. It means killing people," a reader knows that North Korea does not need another apologist; it needs its own Moses, as does Syria, Turkey, the Philippines, and Russia, among so many other places.

Sadly, oppression is often experienced even in countries that are dedicated to liberty, such as the United States. Political systems, government service providers, and businesses that may have the best of intentions can still veer toward the tyrannical if they lack leadership to serve the people instead of being served by them. Now that the reader has been introduced (or reintroduced) to the one leader whom all Jews, Christians, and Muslims recognize as "the Lawgiver," "the Great Deliverer," or, to use the Muslim term, "*rasul Allah*" ("the messenger of God"), the next chapter will focus on how the largest incoming workforce in US history (which is also largest voting bloc) can lead better by employing the Mosaic model and vanquish the would-be Pharaohs at every level in our lives.

THE MOSAIC OF CHAPTER 1

1. The Mosaic model of leadership can be understood from various religious and cultural viewpoints—or strictly as an allegorical story about finding hidden power necessary to fight against oppressive adversity.

2. The Torah (or Pentateuch) refers to the first five books of the Bible—Genesis, Exodus, Leviticus, Numbers, and Deuteronomy—and is commonly printed both as a standalone collection of five and as part of the larger Hebrew Bible (that contains none of the Christian scripture) or as part of the Christian Holy Bible, where it is referred to as the Old Testament. Sometimes the entire Hebrew Bible is referred to as the Torah.
3. The Qur'an was the revelation given to the prophet Muhammed several hundred years later. The instructive stories of the Qur'an and the Christian Bible share fifty characters that are referenced in both sources, and fewer if it is only compared to the Hebrew Bible.
4. The Hadith is the second-highest-ranking book in Islam after the Qur'an.

2

Leadership Models
and Moses

In many Christian traditions, "churchwarden" is the title given to the custodian of the church grounds, a job that ought not to be confused with "janitor." In the Church of England, and later in the Episcopal Church in America, for example, churchwardens have always been non-ordained representatives of the laity—sometimes volunteers, sometimes part-time employees—who function as lay leaders of the parish. Churchwarden is a position of respect that is now open to women as well as men. To be a churchwarden is to be a role model of service.

In an earlier time, when the position was exclusively male, an older churchwarden might be given small, simple sleeping quarters somewhere on the property in exchange for the constant care of the building systems. This is why some people associate churchwardens with retirees or widowers. Typically, a churchwarden-in-residence might have protected the church's sacred spaces, grounds, and any adjacent cemeteries from vandals at night; churchwardens even had recognized, limited municipal police powers to arrest trespassers. The job title is also the origin of the popular smoking device, the "churchwarden pipe."

A churchwarden pipe is characterized by its extra-long stem that keeps the bowls of smoky tobacco away from the faces and out of the eyes of the churchwardens while they tend to their chores. Churchwarden pipes are similar to long clay pipes common in colonial America.

Changing light bulbs, fixing gutters—one might see a churchwarden on a fall afternoon with a leaf rake and his titular pipe fully stoked and clenched between his teeth while getting the property ready for Sunday services. Being a warden of the church had its mundane functions but also its holy importance. The clergy were custodians of the souls of the congregation; churchwardens were the custodians of everything else.

It is this context that Walter Lippmann, an early twentieth-century, two-time Pulitzer Prize–winning journalist, author, and public intellectual, used the word "custodian" regarding leadership when he referenced a "keeper" or a "guardian." Lippmann saw few men and women who understood what it meant to be true leaders, people he described as "the custodians of a nation's ideals, the beliefs it cherishes, of its permanent hopes, of the faith which makes a nation out of a mere aggregation of individuals." Lippmann was a lifelong observer of leadership, especially in the shaping of public opinion. True leaders, according to Lippmann, whether they are permanent or temporary, are custodians in service to a larger group and cause. Conversely, false leaders would be dedicated only to amassing a group that will serve his or her ego. Lippmann is credited with establishing the formal study of leadership dynamics.

Scholarship on the best practices of leadership is crucial because the success of any mission can be doomed from the outset if the leadership is poor or mismatched to the management style that fits the group being led. To organize human resources toward the achievement of a goal, every leader will develop or adopt a management style either by design or by default. According to Edward C. Schleh, in his often-quoted paper in *Management Review*, management style is best understood as the "adhesive that binds diverse operations and functions together. It is the philosophy or set of principles by which you capitalize on the abilities of your people. It is not a procedure on 'how to do,' but is the management framework for doing." Leaders lead through management styles. Every group of people that is organized to do *something*—anything—whether it is to make a profit, make a product, provide a community service, or put on a play—needs to understand the framework on which decisions will be made that affect them.

After World War II, military management models—commonly referred to as the "command-and-control" style—were a natural fit in light of the number of war veterans returning to the workforce. CEOs were spoken of as "generals" who could lead "lieutenants" on campaigns to achieve an organization's "targeted" objectives. In the command-and-control framework, most employees (e.g., any grunt in the army) were expected to focus only on following orders in hopes of being recognized and promoted. By and large, the grunt-level opinion of a mission was immaterial to leadership. To the extent that organizational psychologist and business consultant Rensis Likert is correct when he said that management styles operate on a range between "authoritative" and "participative," large US companies leaned almost exclusively toward the authoritative end of the spectrum for decades.

Most readers today have grown up in the age of the "rockstar," "superstar," or "celebrity" CEO, people such as Lee Iacocca, Jack Welch, Bill Gates, Steve Jobs, Carly Fiorina, or Elon Musk, men and women who are the center of media attention and as well known as the companies with which they are associated. Donald Trump was a self-made major media celebrity and a CEO, but not necessarily a rockstar CEO like others who have been known to turn around the fortunes of companies just by association. The most famous CEOs often appear to affect a stock price based on whether they are staying or leaving a company, such as in the case of Jack Welch.

Welch, chairman and CEO of American multinational conglomerate General Electric from 1981 until his retirement in 2001, oversaw the raising of GE's corporate value by 4,000 percent, according to CBS News. As a popular motivational speaker, Welch cited five basic traits that every organizational leader needed to have: (1) positive energy, (2) ability to energize others, (3) the ability to make tough calls, (4) the talent to execute, and (5) the passion needed to see a project through.

This is consistent with leadership research from the University of Ghent, Belgium. Researchers there describe transformational leaders—the ones who can be effective change-agents—as those who "place value on the development of a clear vision and inspire followers to pursue the vision."

Participative styles of leadership rely on employee intellectual input at every level. Participative leadership had been the cornerstone of Japanese corporate success for decades before it came into vogue in America in the 1970s and 1980s. The four most common participative management styles are (1) collective, (2) democratic, (3) autocratic, and (4) consensus. All participative styles are structured around a higher degree of worker involvement in decision-making than the authoritative styles but with differences in execution.

Separate from the authoritative-participative management-style continuum, the "adaptive" model is another way of leading. Following this framework, every member of a team is trained to be able to perform every function of his or her teammates; if one goes down, or cannot get the job done, the next steps up. Like the command-and-control style, the adaptive method also has military roots. Imagine an elite assault unit attacking an enemy outpost. If part of the unit gets cut off or eliminated and cannot reach the objective, the other team members must adapt seamlessly to the changed conditions.

Although the Qur'an states that God had granted Moses "good health, strength, knowledge, and wisdom" and that the "weak and oppressed turned to him for protection and justice," by all appearances, it would seem that Moses' leadership skills were dormant for much of his life. Eventually, Moses would develop a leadership model hitherto unseen in history, but he was a "slow starter." Despite identifying as an Israelite, Moses hid behind his privilege. Yet, as an indulged "prince" of Egypt fleeing from responsibility for a man's death—even if it was self-defense—Moses' story is evidence that one's past may not always predict one's destiny.

Frequently, in the daily news media, one sees stories of ordinary people who have become extraordinary leaders. It could be a young

Considerable scholarship has been done on leadership models, and these four examples are in no way a comprehensive list. To understand the difference that servant leadership attempts to make, however, it is important for people who are unfamiliar with leadership studies to have a brief background.

In (1) the collective model, for example, employees who are empowered to make decisions for the company are assigned specific responsibilities to research and investigate and then bring their conclusions to the collective ruling group. Before implementation, the collective accepts responsibility for those decisions, but that is distinguished from (2) the democratic style of participation, in which the employees "vote" (more or less) on important issues before a manager above the group decides to accept, adapt, or reject that outcome. In the democratic style, the manager's decision and recommendations are then sent back to the group, which would begin deliberations again based on the manager's decision—and so on—until an agreement with the manager is reached.

The (3) autocratic participative style may sound like a contradiction in terms, but it is common in smaller companies because resolutions can be reached more quickly than in other participative models. In this case, the employee buy-in comes at the early "brainstorming" level regarding the organizational problems of proposed solutions, but after the recommendations are kicked up to management, the final decision—and the ramifications of the decision—are shouldered only by the leader. Finally, in (4) the consensus model, a simple majority of the participants settles each issue presented. Those who held minority opinions are expected to be good sports until the next decision-making process begins.

teenager or senior citizen spontaneously taking charge after a tragedy, a survivor of a gang culture who has become a job provider, or a timid politician who becomes the unlikely voice of an aggrieved group. In each case, an inherent but perhaps dormant ability to assess and respond to a call to leadership when necessity knocked saved the day.

But leadership is a complex phenomenon, and not all leaders succeed in the long run. Some people become victims of their own egos; some confuse service with entitlement; others might just break under the pressure of scrutiny. It may all come down to how well prepared one must be in advance of the opportunity. The more one learns about Moses, the more the old maxim holds: "Fortune favors the prepared mind."

In the same way that Moses was uniquely suited to be an agent for change because he had grown up around the same royal Egyptians whom he would later challenge, any of us can be effective in our own communities if we are willing to be a part of a miracle. Sometimes the most miraculous thing we can do is overcome our own insecurities.

Instead of a disgraced, entitled prince on the run from justice, God saw something else in Moses as he grew in his experience as a shepherd. In a simple act of tenderness, a gesture of loving reassurance to a powerless creature, God detected the main quality in Moses required to perform the superhuman act of liberating the Hebrew slaves from Egyptian bondage: *humility*. Moses may have had strength, stamina, knowledge, and wisdom, but God determined humility was the personal characteristic that a liberator would need most to convince the Israelites to follow him, disarm Pharaoh long enough to get God's people out the door, and then lead the refugees through the desert to a new home that would be their reward after generations of suffering.

If it is true that character is what one reveals when no one is watching, then humility is a virtue one would never see as a public act. Obviously, bragging about one's humbleness defeats the whole purpose. To those who believe in an omniscient God, there would be no point in faking humility in private, either. Both the Bible and the Qur'an contain many stories about Moses' manners and his deep respect for others in

Early midrashic commentary predated the use of "rabbi" in Judaism. Instead, the commentators were known then as "sages." Midrash's distinct philological purpose intends to "fill the gaps" in both the Hebrew Bible and the Haggadah using literary critical methods such as examining oddities in word choices as well as what has been left out. Midrash looks for parallels in other texts, particularly when the Bible and the Haggadah tell the same story.

For example, the Exodus from Egypt is told every year at the Passover table in a book called the Haggadah. The book consists of prayers, stories, and songs that allow the participants to experience the drama of the liberation from Egypt and the saga of a people who transition from slavery to freedom and leave an idol-worshiping society oppressed by a despot to become a free people in their own land.

What is remarkable about the Haggadah is that the main character of the story is only mentioned once in passing rather than being given full credit for performing one of the greatest acts of human liberation in history, delivering divine law to the newly freed people, and bringing them to the Promised Land.

Many explanations have been offered for this puzzling omission. What we do know about the genesis of the Haggadah is that it developed over time after the Jews lost their sovereignty in the land of Israel to the Romans and were hard pressed to preserve their faith in God surrounded by idol-worshiping people. The sages of the era must have gone out of their way to emphasize that the miracle of the liberation, the giving of the law, and the return to the Promised Land was an act of God rather than man and that Moses was only a vessel used by God to make the divine will known to the world.

his heart, but perhaps the best, most instructive example of Moses' sincere humility is found in the Midrash.

"Midrash" is a Hebrew word derived from a verb meaning "to inquire" or "to seek out" and is both the name of the scholarly process and the oldest book of Jewish commentary on the Torah. Midrash often challenges the literal meaning of a text by making logical inferences from what is stated or from what the text leaves out. Midrash does not just read between the lines of the Bible; it *writes* them. The rabbinic Midrash commentary on Moses that is known as Exodus Rabbah adds this story:

> Once, while Moses our Teacher was tending Jethro's sheep, one of the lambs ran away. Moses ran after it until it reached a small, shaded place. There, the lamb came across a pool and began to drink. As Moses approached the lamb, he said, "I did not know you ran away because you were thirsty. You are so exhausted!" The Holy One said, "Since you tend people's sheep with such overwhelming love, I swear you shall be the shepherd of My sheep, Israel."

This non-biblical passage reflects the rabbinic wisdom that a true leader is not interested in seeking power. Rather, he or she realizes that there is an important task to be done and accepts the responsibility of leadership despite his or her misgivings about assuming so much authority. One great lesson of Moses' life, then, is the most effective leaders are not ego focused. Moses did not "need to lead" to fill some part of his soul or compensate for a past tragedy, and he was not looking to become a leader for life. Anybody who needs to be the leader at all times—for the rest of their lives—is probably very insecure about how harshly they will be judged once they are no longer able to control their former underlings. These people may best be avoided until they learn the custodial aspects of leadership.

The midrashic story of Moses tending his flocks of sheep and goats also illustrates that, at its core, leadership potential is inherent at some level in every human being and may shine when called upon in situa-

The Hebrew Bible, the Christian Holy Bible, and the Qur'an specify that Moses was a shepherd tending Jethro's flocks of sheep
and goats, but in the Hebrew Midrash, the story of Moses' compassion to lost sheep is told this way: "Our rabbis taught: When
Moses our Master and Teacher peace be upon him was shepherding Jethro's flock in the desert, a kid (or young goat) ran away, so
Moses pursued him until he reached a shelter."

As a result, it is common for Jews to picture an immature goat
at this most crucial part of the Moses narrative. Further disconti-
nuity arises with the casual scholar, however, when the Exodus
Rabbah from the Midrash is translated into English because then
the animal in question is often described as a little lamb.

tions big and small. The Prophet Muhammed is reported to have said,
"All of you are guardians, and all guardians are responsible for their
subjects." To the extent that William Shakespeare was correct when he
wrote in Act III, scene I of *Henry IV*, "Heavy is the head that wears the
crown," some people feel no burden from being the custodian of the
hopes and dreams of others, and they step in and out of that role naturally, selflessly, and effortlessly.

So, Moses appears to be in a category of naturally gifted custodians
who shy from positions of power and need to be nudged into leadership. Moses' servanthood was the basis for the management style he was
developing without even being aware of it. Unseen forces were conspir-
ing to make Moses understand his destiny. Without intending it, Moses
had been preparing himself for leadership; Egypt, without knowing it,
was preparing itself for the return of Moses. The climactic events began
with the death of a pharaoh who had been like a father figure to Moses
at one time and the ascension to the throne of the new pharaoh to whom
Moses once had been like a brother:

During that long period, the king of Egypt died. The Israelites groaned in their slavery and cried out, and their cry for help because of their slavery went up to God. God heard their groaning and he remembered his covenant with Abraham, with Isaac and with Jacob. So God looked on the Israelites and was concerned about them. (Exodus 2:23–25)

Meanwhile, Moses' life was comfortable. His death warrant in Egypt had expired with the passing of Pharaoh. With Jethro's daughter, Zipporah, Moses had fathered one son, Gershom (a name given to signify Moses' self-awareness that he had become "a stranger in a strange land"), and very likely another boy named Eliezer. The timelines given in the Qur'an and the Bible concerning the period that Moses spent shepherding with the Midianites do not sync up, as the former says that ten years passed in Midian, but Exodus in the Bible states that Moses was eighty years old when he confronted the new pharaoh, which is about a thirty-year difference.

Any quarrel over how much time Moses spent in Midian is largely a distraction. Veteran readers of ancient texts are accustomed to looking at numbers symbolically. Moses had matured in Midian, he had been gone a long time from Egypt, he had become an experienced shepherd for his father-in-law, he was still faithful, and there were no more mentions of outbursts of anger. Regardless of how old Moses actually was, the importance of achieving personal equanimity is the lesson for the reader. The Qur'an specifies that after the killing of the overseer, God forgave Moses and, as one qur'anic commentator described it, "Moses began to show more patience and sympathy toward people." This kind of peace can come to people at different ages. While tending sheep as a stranger in a strange land with some sort of speech impairment about which he was embarrassed, Moses had completely submitted to the responsibility of providing security, health, prosperity, and sustenance through quiet, strong leadership to his flock of sheep, family, and other tribe members without seeking the trappings of power.

According to Rabbi Yaacov Halevi Pilber, a Rosh Yeshiva (head of an Orthodox academy) in Israel, this submission of Moses comprised the three most important qualities a leader should have: (1) be a good shepherd of people, (2) be trustworthy, and (3) be humble. In Arabic, the word for submission is "Islam." In the fourteenth-century Muslim commentary *Stories of the Prophets* by renowned qur'anic scholar Ibn Kathir, Moses' life with the Midianites is described like this:

> It was a period of major preparation. Certainly Moses's mind was absorbed in the stars every night. He followed the sunrise and the sunset every day. He pondered on the plant and how it splits the soil and appears thereafter. He contemplated water and how the earth is revived by it and flourishes after its death. . . . In addition to physical preparation, there was a similar spiritual preparation. It was made in complete seclusion, in the middle of the desert, and in the places of pasture. Silence was his way of life, and seclusion was his vehicle. Allah the Almighty prepared for His prophet the tools he would need later on to righteously bear the commands of Allah the Exalted.

Ibn Kathir's *Stories of the Prophets* introduces qur'anic narratives and commentary to early Islamic readers and non-Muslims alike. As a testament to Ibn Kathir's success and the quality of the scholarship, people interested in the Qur'an often start with this fourteenth-century work that includes elements of history, exegesis, and comparative literature.

Yet Moses' life at this point may not be as extraordinary as it seems. Historical figures often are elevated for the same life choices we all make. For example, at around forty years old, Moses was much older than most Americans when he left home for the first time. The land called Midian was a hike on foot, for sure, but, as the crow flies, not that far from his boyhood palace in Egypt. Most young people in the United States move much farther away for college, to find work, or when they marry somebody from a different state (or from another country). Millennial men, in particular, have been tarred with a reputation for enjoying the comforts of home too long, also known as a "failure to launch." The Moses story affirms that it's never too late to aspire to leadership and achieve greatness and that, by a modern metric, Millennials have nothing to be ashamed about if they take a while to find their true calling.

Regarding Moses' preparation, as Ibn Kathir makes clear, Moses spent his years in isolation learning about the world around him, understanding the vastness of the universe, more at peace with simplicity than with the indulgences of life. Some modern critics might dismiss Moses' pastoral years as "navel gazing" or "tree hugging," or even just aimless, but the Qur'an states that those years of solitary contemplation were not wasted at all. Perhaps the opulence of the palace and the austerity of the wilderness had been the only preparation he needed for what was ahead. In both cases—living with the royal family and living with the Midianites—Moses remained a devoted God follower even in non-Hebrew communities.

Scholars of literature or philosophy also might recognize Moses' interest in the interconnectedness of the universe as predating the nineteenth-century transcendental movement. Transcendentalists such a Ralph Waldo Emerson engaged in a conversation between theology and science; Moses' extended residency in the Midianite wilderness is not dissimilar to Henry David Thoreau's contemplative sabbatical in a hut on the shores of Emerson's Walden Pond in Massachusetts. Maybe Millennials who have been in no rush to get driver's licenses, finish college, or buy homes are tapping into the same state of mind that Moses grew to appreciate too—and maybe this is why it took God's voice coming out of flaming shrubbery, the miracle of the burning bush, to shock Moses out of his comfort.

First, a sidebar to the nonreligious reader, a concession and an explanation about the use of the word "miracles": Most people would agree that Moses talking to God through a flame sounds like something from *Harry Potter*. Even worse, Moses does not just take orders from a burning bush; he also argues with it! But such is the notion of miracles in holy texts. Based on the Latin root word for "to see or behold," the word that comes down to us into English as "miracle" is in the "diminutive" form (note the suffix -cle) and implies "a little something wondrous to see."

A miracle does not require a suspension of disbelief or, even more so, a suspension of the laws of physics, but rather the willingness to behold something extraordinary and appreciate it for what it is. Perhaps the following anecdote will help. In seminary circles, dozens of people vouch for the authenticity of this exchange (which probably means it did not happen).

A famous, highly respected German theologian was giving a lecture about the book of Genesis at the University of Chicago in the 1950s. At the point when the story turned to the temptation of Eve by the serpent in the Garden of Eden, a young man raised his hand in incredulity: "Professor, are you here to tell us that you are interested in talking snakes?" To which the German theologian reportedly replied, "Dear boy, I am not interested in a talking snake; I'm interested in what the snake had to say." And so it might just be with discussions of miracles in the chapters ahead.

For the time being, Judeo-Christian tradition and Islam agree largely on the elements in the story of how Moses was called to leadership—just not on the order. In each account there is a mountain, a mysterious flame through which God speaks, and a call to leadership. The Qur'an says that one day, while shepherding, Moses became vaguely homesick and then suddenly decided he wanted to take a family road trip back to see the old neighborhood in Egypt. Moses himself did not know what got into him; it's just a compulsion he cannot resist. He tells Zipporah to pack up the kid(s), and they leave the next day. But Moses gets lost along the way (this happens a lot to Moses, apparently), and the travelers find themselves at Mount Tur, near Mount Sinai in the southern part of the Arab Peninsula, not really near Egypt at all.

At the foot of Mount Tur, Moses sees a mysterious fire in the distance that he sets out to investigate in hopes of determining where he is and/or bringing back a burning branch to warm his family. He has an expectation that something about the effort will be rewarding but no vision of what he was about to encounter. According to the Qur'an, "As he neared the fire, he heard a sonorous voice calling him: 'O Moses, I am Allah, the Lord of the Universe.'"

The Qur'an does not explain what about the fire that drew Moses was so mysterious, nor does it preclude the flame emanated from or near a bush. Muslims do not quibble about the expression "a burning bush experience"; it is just one of the many common phrases from the Judeo-Christian narrative that has made its way into everyday speech around the world. According to the Bible, it goes like this:

> Now Moses was tending the flock of Jethro, his father-in-law, the priest of Midian, and he led the flock to the far side of the wilderness and came to Horeb, the mountain of God. There the angel of the Lord appeared to him in flames of fire from within a bush. Moses saw that though the bush was on fire, it did not burn up. So Moses thought, "I will go over and see this strange sight—why the bush does not burn up."
>
> When the Lord saw that he had gone over to look, God called to him from within the bush, "Moses! Moses!"
>
> And Moses said, "Here I am."
>
> "Do not come any closer," God said. "Take off your sandals, for the place where you are standing is holy ground." Then he said, "I am the God of your father, the God of Abraham, the God of Isaac and the God of Jacob." At this, Moses hid his face, because he was afraid to look at God.
>
> The Lord said, "I have indeed seen the misery of my people in Egypt. I have heard them crying out because of their slave drivers, and I am concerned about their suffering. So I have come down to rescue them from the hand of the Egyptians and to bring them up out of that land into a good and spacious land, a land flowing with milk and honey—the home of the Canaanites, Hittites, Amorites, Perizzites, Hivites and Jebusites. And now the cry of the Israelites has reached me, and I have seen the way the Egyptians are oppressing them. So now, go. I am sending you to Pharaoh to bring my people, the Israelites, out of Egypt."

In Islam, God's instructions after that are fairly simple. To paraphrase, God tells Moses to go to Pharaoh and his chiefs (to whom God refers as "an evil gang" that has "transgressed all bounds"), and it will all work out, trust me.

Putting aside for the time being any rightful quarrels about how the Canaanites, Hittites, Amorites, Perizzites, Hivites, and Jebusites were all about to be displaced, the narrative of God commanding Moses—an ordinary person chosen for a specific purpose at a specific time in his life—underscores the possibility that any person might be called to service if he or she is deemed worthy. The qur'anic narrative also does not indicate that Moses was conscious of any special status when he accepted his assignment; he was simply convinced that the "sonorous voice" deserved his obedience. Interestingly, although the Qur'an's version of the story agrees with the Bible about Moses being required to remove his sandals as he approached the fire, for the place where he was standing was holy ground, only Muslim worship protocol demands the removal of all shoes when entering any modern house of worship such as a mosque. No such practice is observed in Judaism or Christianity.

Some Sunday School wags have suggested that if God spoke to all of us through a burning bush that was not consumed by the flames, no one would ever need faith in God because everybody would have proof; proof of God renders faith unnecessary. Disbelief is not the opposite of belief, however—it is the other side of the same coin. Even among believers, moments of disbelief create further prayerful conversation. Moses had been worshiping an all-powerful deity his whole life—the true God of all other gods—but even after obvious evidence in this burning bush that his faith had not been misplaced, Moses still wanted more:

> Then Moses answered and said, "But suppose they will not believe me or listen to my voice; suppose they say, 'The Lord has not appeared to you.'"
> So the Lord said to him, "What *is* that in your hand?"
> He said, "A rod."

And God said, "Cast it on the ground." So Moses cast it on the ground, and it became a serpent; and Moses fled from it. Then the Lord said to Moses, "Reach out your hand and take *it* by the tail" (and he reached out his hand and caught it, and it became a rod in his hand), "that they may believe that the Lord God of their fathers, the God of Abraham, the God of Isaac, and the God of Jacob, has appeared to you."

After that, according to the Qur'an and the Bible, God instructed Moses to put his hand inside his cloak—the Qur'an actually specifies the Arabic word for "armpit"—and withdraw it. When Moses pulled it out, the flesh of the hand was white and leprous, but after putting it back in again, it was made whole. The Qur'an states, "You have two signs from Your Lord; go to Pharaoh and his chiefs, for they are an evil gang and have transgressed all bounds." This is the point when Moses overcame his awe and accepted that God was calling him to leadership.

But this is where things get kind of complicated in the Bible account. First, God assures Moses that when he meets with the elders of Israel, they will listen to him and they will have his back when Moses confronts Pharaoh about their treatment. Then God tells Moses to ask Pharaoh to allow the Israelites to cease working long enough to take a three-day journey into the desert to offer animal sacrifices to God. Don't think "Burning Man"; think "Burning Menu." Presumably, that meant all 600,000 Israelites being allowed to hike three days into the desert, have a food festival in honor of the Lord, and then travel three days back to work for a total of one week off. But as God explains to Moses, "When you return to Egypt, see that you perform before Pharaoh all the wonders I have given you the power to do. But I will harden his heart so that he will not let the people go." For good reason, this biblical passage, which seems to suggest God is setting up Pharaoh only to knock him down later on, has always been controversial. What did God mean by "I will harden his heart"?

Some critics point out that Moses might have been able to persuade Pharaoh to let the Israelites go, but God wanted to make an example of Pharaoh, so he "hardened his heart" to create the excuse necessary to wipe out innocent lives. This is proof, as that cynical argument goes, that God is a self-admitted, cold-blooded murderer. Yet there is no full agreement on what exactly "harden his heart" means and whether it was just another Hebrew idiom such as "broken heart" and "putting words in somebody's mouth," both of which started in the Bible, but neither of which are taken literally. In support of those who insist on an abstract interpretation, a few verses later, the text also says Pharaoh himself *hardened his own heart*. So what is God doing that Pharaoh can apparently do himself?

For rabbis, even after millennia of debate, there is no simple answer. Because the comment does not appear in the Qur'an, Muslim scholarship is of limited value here, and many Jewish and Christian scholars just punt the question. Some may chalk it up to the ineffable mystery of God with a shrug. In a blog post titled "Who Really Hardened Pharaoh's Heart?" by Rabbi Danya Ruttenberg, for example, the claim is made that due to his repeated cruelties to the Israelites, "Pharaoh sealed his own fate, for himself and his relationship with God." That may be true, but is it enough to satisfy the people who are uncomfortable with God's promise to game the outcome of Moses' showdown with Pharaoh by forcing the king to be unreceptive?

Perhaps the easiest explanation is a reconsideration of the expression. The Bible contains many Hebrew idioms, many of whose *exact* meanings have been lost over time, such as in the book of Ruth when the titular character was instructed to ignite the passions of the older Boaz by "uncovering his feet" as he slept off some wine. Should the expression be taken literally, or is the word "feet" a euphemistic stand-in for "lower extremities" (*wink, wink*)?

Acknowledging this situation might go a long way toward understanding the true meaning of "hardening his heart." If God is truly omniscient, God already knows that Pharaoh is going to obstruct Moses' efforts to free the Jews; if Pharaoh is a typical tyrant, he may delay announcing his decision in order to draw more attention to himself. In this context, "hardening Pharaoh's heart" infers that God was merely forcing

Pharaoh to give Moses an answer instead of dragging it out. Pharaoh could have responded to Moses' demand to "Let my people go!" with a "Let my people think about it!" answer and just left it there. Perhaps every time Pharaoh did not harden his own heart against the Hebrews, God stepped in. An edict such as this would be consistent with God's desire to release the Israelites from bondage as fast as possible.

That theory might get an "amen" from office workers who toil under a tyrannical boss. The better the idea from the floor, the more powerful the proposal from a young executive, the longer some poor leaders take to make a decision. Egomaniac bosses need to make themselves the center of attention at all times. Many earnest, dutiful employees might wish they, too, could harden their own boss's heart just to be put out of the misery of waiting for an answer.

Then again, if any of us who could see ourselves the way God sees us, perhaps the tyrants in our lives would never be any kind of obstacle at all. When we have confidence in our competence, we feel more empowered to take on seemingly impossible tasks. Like Moses, however, it frequently takes an outsider's perspective to see what is going on within us. For example, a "higher power" in an organization can determine leadership qualities merely by observing to whom employees naturally turn for advice or want to keep in their network. Workers with a history of their peers turning to them to represent their grievances to superiors or to seek advice already have been picked as a leader through an organic selection. When there is tension in the workplace, this process can be accelerated. In times of tyrants, informal leaders may find themselves growing in prominence due to their attractive emotional intelligence. Such a person may even resist being called to leadership; family members, coworkers, and neighbors may insist that he or she step forward whether they like it or not.

This is why "burning bush" moments come in different forms at different times for different people. It may be a sense of panic has inflamed an organization after a manager surprisingly "crashed and burned" under their workload or due to a personal crisis, or when the sudden responsibilities of another mouth to feed at home lights a fire under a young mother or father to be more productive. A burning bush may not appear miraculous at all; the call to leadership could come by the coffee machine, the water cooler, or a company softball game. When the call to leadership comes from higher up, it might be disguised as something practical such as the chance to return to school, move within a company, or enter into a management training program.

This is true because, in the qur'anic narrative, Moses was drawn to a burning bush in the desert for fairly practical reasons: to figure out where he was and/or warm his family because he was a good custodian of his wife and kids. Yet just by being a good steward of others, he was actually answering an invitation to be a part of the greatest organizational turnaround in human history. And while Moses might have been overcome by his customary humility for a moment, once he seemingly accepted the promotion from shepherd to prophet, the subject then pivoted to the team that Moses felt he would need to be most successful.

Any successful business undertaking depends on a regular inventory check. The best leaders perform similar inventories of their own strengths and weaknesses as they correspond to a task at hand. An objective assessment of one's own limitations as a leader might prompt a much-needed delegation to another, better-suited teammate. True leaders are not threatened by the talents of others because assembling a team that brings complementary and diverse skills to the table is part of what a good leader does. There is no shame in not being able to do everything equally well; it is shameful to allow one's ego to get in the way of a successful mission.

Although the Bible explains, "The man Moses was the humblest of all men on the face of the earth" (Numbers 12:3), this humility also meant Moses was keenly aware of his own shortcomings. To be God's prophetic spokesperson to Pharaoh, almost ironically, Moses felt he needed a better spokesperson than himself. Anybody who has had to stand in front of a room to make an important presentation can relate to fretting over their weight, their clothes, their stature, or a prominent facial or physical feature. According to the Qur'an, Moses' biggest insecurity was the way he talked:

> Moses said: "O my Lord! Open for me my chest (grant me self-confidence, contentment, and boldness). And ease my task for me; and make loose the knot (the defect) from my tongue, (remove the incorrectness of my speech) that they understand my speech, and appoint for me a helper from my family, Aaron, my brother."

Did Moses stutter? Did he have a lisp, a hairlip, or did he slur his s-words like Daffy Duck? It is a biblical mystery. The qur'anic reference to a "knot" could imply "scanning speech," medically referred to as ataxic dysarthria, a kind of halting vocal pattern where the syllables of each word are interrupted unpredictably by pauses of varying lengths. Of course, "my tongue is in knots" could have meant what it still means today: that somebody is at a loss for words when they get nervous. With all his time spent alone in the wilderness, it would be fair to assert that Moses was an introvert; maybe he simply became tongue-tied when he was not around friends or family.

The account in the Bible, however, seems to indicate that Moses' affliction was more profound than mere shyness; it was a lack of eloquence. Unlike the Qur'an, in Exodus, it is God's idea to enlist Moses' brother Aaron. To the point of annoyance for God in the hiring process, God even had to give Moses an extra push to assume his life's mission:

> Moses said to the Lord, "Pardon your servant, Lord. I have never been eloquent, neither in the past nor since you have spoken to your servant. I am slow of speech and tongue."
>
> The Lord said to him, "Who gave human beings their mouths? Who makes them deaf or mute? Who gives them sight or makes them blind? Is it not I, the Lord? Now go; I will help you speak and will teach you what to say."
>
> But Moses said, "Pardon your servant, Lord. Please send someone else."

Then the Lord's anger burned against Moses and the Lord said, "What about your brother, Aaron the Levite? I know he can speak well. He is already on his way to meet you, and he will be glad to see you. You shall speak to him and put words in his mouth; I will help both of you speak and will teach you what to do. He will speak to the people for you, and it will be as if he were your mouth and as if you were God to him. But take this staff in your hand so you can perform the signs with it."

Of all the many exchanges between God and God's people in the Bible, this one may resonate most with any manager looking to promote a talented protégé. Despite all that had been shown to Moses, God is frustrated at not being able to close the deal. The implied tone and the end result are almost comical. In other words, God says, "I need you to take this job. I'm under deadline." After Moses humbly demurs again, God suggests, "Don't you have a brother who's a pretty good talker? Bring him. I'll tell you what to say, you'll tell him, and he'll make the pitch. Do we have a deal now? Oh, and, uh, don't forget your stick. You're going to need that."

But there might be other reasons for Moses' insistence on enlisting his brother on the project. Presumably, Aaron and Moses had been apart ever since Moses fled to Midian. This implies that Aaron had continued to live in Egyptian bondage in Moses' absence, continued to suffer under Pharaoh, and maintained his own status as a respected elder among the Hebrews.

Before Moses could confront Pharaoh, Moses knew his first mission would be to get the Israelites to accept him as their new leader, and this is where Aaron's decades of "street cred" could be useful. Anybody who has been asked by an organization to take over a new territory likely has experienced an awkward cultural transition to new surroundings. A young teacher moving into a new school district, a regional sales manager assuming control of some extra branch offices, or a member of the clergy following a call to a faraway synagogue/church/mosque all know that the success or failure of any new endeavor often depends on a nuanced understanding of how leaders will connect to the way a particular group identifies itself. A book-smart young executive might be wise to bring an older, friendlier, easily relatable social performer to build a bridge to the new company—and vice versa.

Never mind that Moses' Egyptian-speaking skills had to be at least a little rusty, too.

Sigmund Freud, the founder of psychoanalysis, in his book *Moses and Monotheism*, argues that Moses was an Egyptian rather than a Hebrew. Like Karl Marx, Freud was a secular Jew who lost his faith as a child growing up in Vienna, Austria, where he saw a Viennese anti-Semite humiliate his father in public while walking in the street.

Unlike Moses, who confronted an Egyptian taskmaster humiliating a Hebrew slave, Freud instead came to the same conclusion as Marx: religion, which originally was meant to curb the violent instincts of society, had become an irrelevant illusion that did more harm than good. Both Freud and Marx advocated for reason and science to take the place of religion in the public consciousness.

Freud went ever further when he described religion as a neurosis, a form of irrational behavior. After World War I, which devastated Europe and resulted in thousands of soldiers suffering from shell shock and needing treatment, Freud's psychoanalysis became enormously popular. But here again, as in the case of Marx, monotheistic religion has survived both Marxism and the Freudian view of Moses and monotheism.

The last any of the Children of Israel had seen of Moses was as a de facto palace-prince-turned-escaped-killer. With Aaron as his hype man, Moses would be able to get the Israelites to accept him faster than if he were on his own. This is also important to note because people who bring some of their own past colleagues with them into a new company are often perceived as better leaders than those who arrive alone. The popular theory here is if others quit their jobs to follow somebody else into uncertainty, they must not be that bad. The popular business expression "People quit leaders, not companies" is the other side of the coin to the truism that it is harder to find a great leader than a great company.

In an article about leadership, *Forbes Magazine* once identified that the best leaders "share the harvest of their success to help build momentum for those around them." Rabbi Avraham Yitzchak HaLevi Kilav suggests that Moses may have been similarly mindful about family birth order. As the younger brother, Moses' insistence that he needed Aaron at his side could have been another demonstration of his gentle kindness regarding the feelings of others. According to the Midrash Tanchumah on Exodus 27, Moses was ready to go to Pharaoh, but he refused to bypass his brother, who had been prophesying for years. The best leaders share the spotlight. A strong will to succeed at a righteous cause will be the fuel that Moses will use to achieve the goal, not his ego. Trustworthy leaders not only refuse to make promises they cannot keep but also do not bypass others unnecessarily or prevent them from achieving their own personal advancement.

One hallmark of effective leadership is the refusal to waste too much time lamenting the lack of better tools or resenting the people with other skill sets needed to accomplish a goal. Moses sets a pretty good example of doing "the best you can, where you are, with what you got." Quickly overcoming his initial resistance, Moses just went with it and never looked back. At the start of any new venture, optimizing research has its place, but it can also create "analysis paralysis." God used the humility of a prophet to attack the arrogance of a tyrant in order to teach a lesson to the world, and Moses and Aaron got right to it. Would the results of their efforts have changed if Moses and Aaron had conducted a series of focus groups to determine an event horizon and followed a corporate action plan? Sometimes nothing beats accepting the trade-off of going with your gut over prolonged deliberation.

It should be noted, by the way, that just because Moses and Aaron were male, it does not mean that the original story of the exodus of the Jews from Egypt is completely androcentric. Miriam, the older sister of Aaron and Moses who arranged for Moses' mother to be his wet nurse, is later granted the status of God's prophet in the Jewish and Christian traditions after she plays a prominent role in the success of the parting of the Red Sea. In Christianity, Miriam—the Hebrew form of "Mary"—is also celebrated as one of "The Three Great Marys of the Bible" along with Mary, mother of Jesus, and Mary Magdalene, Christ's dedicated follower who selflessly and humbly provided support and loyalty.

In the context of the time, and in consonance with the selection of previous messengers, that Moses was a male shepherd would have been customary. However, anybody can be called to leadership, and the model of Moses' interaction with God would be equally acceptable for a woman leader or even a person who does not believe in the divine nature of a burning bush. If one were an atheist, however, one would not have to admit that the burning bush is divine in order to consider what the bush has to say.

Looking at the narrative more abstractly, People of Go(o)d should never tolerate the forced exploitation of others anywhere at any time. Even when seeing the Moses story only as an allegory, the crux of the conflict still resonates: marginalized people were being oppressed, an opportunity to speak truth to power had been presented, and assistance beyond one's own power base was evident. Any leader—man or woman, faithful or not—will see nonreligious parallels of the Moses story in their own experience. In the context of today and in consonance with modern times, any humble person could be called to be the *next* Moses.

For example, perhaps not surprisingly, thousands of years after the events of the Bible and the Qur'an, humility as a premium quality of leadership is the subject of fresh research. In the article "Bringing Humility to Leadership: Antecedents and Consequences of Leader Humility," authors J. Andrew Morris, Céleste M. Brotheridge, and John C. Urbanski argue that the "romanticized notion of celebrity CEOs that has been lionized in the popular business press has its place in the leadership pantheon, but, like any other approach to leadership, has limitations in its application."

Instead—and as almost a reaction to the celebrity CEO model that defined this last generation of business leaders—a new perception has grown that measures the success of organizational leadership over a longer term and on different scales of corporate return. This new model, business researchers argue, posits that the leaders of tomorrow will possess strong personal will *and* humility in equal measures, almost the antithesis of the rockstar CEO model and the "I alone can fix it" philosophy.

If it is true that every generation is, to some degree, a reaction to the generation that came before it, we should not be surprised to see that Millennial interest in humble leadership might be the antidote to the damage done by a more callous class of some Baby Boomer and Gen X media influencers who have encouraged social division if it helps to achieve their desired political or social goals. These harsh voices of discord that were decried by Senator John McCain of Arizona before his death seem to relish promoting populist policies under which only one group of Americans will win. For example, some of those talk media forces are so ugly and racist that they can only be called wicked. That said, many hurtful policies of the past few years that seemed focused on scapegoating already disempowered groups while enriching others may not have been sprung from an overtly evil intent—just cynicism, the general lack of faith in (or hope for) the entire human species.

Separating families seeking legal migration at the US southern border, for example, appeared to be predicated on the assumption that most Americans simply would not care about the abuse of brown-skinned people because it did not affect the average American. As the cynical reasoning goes, if family separation deterred other Central American refugees from attempting legal or illegal migration, then a greater good would be achieved. In their own minds, the White House policymakers and immigration enforcement officials even judged family separation as the *most* "humane" treatment to the "problem" in the long run. There is ample polling data that suggested these policies resonated with a portion of the electorate. Fortunately, faced with the real-life images of the emotional and financial cost of that cynicism, many previous supporters later drew the line at terrorizing children. The courts agreed.

Perhaps more than at any other time in US history, however, cynicism has been allowed to pass for wisdom in much of our public discourse. Eternally, pessimism and optimism—opposing poles of our day-to-day outlook on life—have been locked in a cycle. But cynicism is rarely wise, and it is almost always a product of lazy thinking. Ideas like "people never change" or "society just isn't as good as it used to be; things will never get better, we just have to accept that" are symptoms of a fatigued mind-set that almost guarantees the self-fulfilling prophecy of failure. Because of this, a cynic's jaundiced hopelessness limits his or her creative imagination of the future just when new ways of thinking or fresh approaches to old problems are needed most. Restoring a better balance to leadership is an opportunity for next-generation leaders who are focused on doing well and doing good.

In the qur'anic version of the Moses narrative per Ibn Kathir, Allah seems to speak directly to the importance of resisting cynicism and not giving up in the middle of a tough challenge. In instructing Moses, God says, "Go, you and your brother, with My Ayat (proofs, lessons, verses, evidences, signs, revelations, etc.), and do not, you both, slacken and become weak in My Remembrance." Unlike the biblical version that claims God knows everything that is about to happen, the qur'anic narrative seems to imply that the future may be unwritten: "Go, both of you, to Pharaoh, verily, he has transgressed all bounds in disbelief and disobedience and behaved as an arrogant and as a tyrant. And speak to him mildly, perhaps he may accept admonition or fear Allah."

Regardless of what Pharaoh does, though, God says that Moses must remain steady and focused. A Bible lesson by Rabbi Pilber uses the Talmud, an ancient book of Jewish instruction and rabbinical scholarship, to articulate this point about imbalanced leadership. In *Tractate Berachot*, Rabbi Yehoshua and Rabbi Gamaliel are talking when the former says to the latter, "Woe to the generation whose *provider* you are, and woe to the ship whose *captain* you are." A true leader needs both qualities—provider and captain. As provider, the true leader takes care of the needs of each individual under his or her care. And as a captain, he or she steers the ship of state safely through all sorts of weather from shore to shore.

The captain and provider for the ideals, beliefs, and hopes of others is the same custodian of Lippman's definition of a true leader. Moses had both qualities. According to the Midrash, in a story not found in the Torah, Rabbi Pilber recounts how when Moses was still in the older Pharaoh's court as a younger man, he would go out secretly to witness Hebrew suffering. One time, Moses "saw a small person carrying a heavy load, and a big person carrying a small load and so on. And so he rearranged the loads." He was not above it all, but rather behaved like a provider who personally helped each person and also cared for the entire community, as a captain does. When he saw the slaves were given no rest, he said to the older Pharaoh later, "He who has a slave who does not rest, the slave will die of exhaustion." The older Pharaoh told him, "Give them a day of rest," and so Moses was able to give the Hebrew slaves the Sabbath day to rest.

This early negotiation with the older Pharaoh foreshadows both the later pivotal saving of the thirsty lamb that God observed and the confrontation with the cruel son of the older Pharaoh that Moses was about to have now that he had his team together. As promised, the Bible explains how the Lord directed Aaron to meet up with Moses at Mount Horeb, where the two had a touching, brotherly reunion. Moses brought Aaron up to speed on everything the Lord had sent him to say, and he even showed Aaron how he could change his staff into a snake. Moses also did the hand-in-the-cloak thing. In turn, Aaron brought together all Israelite elders and did the talking for Moses as the prophet repeated the snake and the hand miracles. They, too, were convinced that this humble servant of God was sent to lead them. The elders believed the Lord had heard their cries and seen their misery, and because they felt so cared for, they bowed down and worshiped God.

Moses' innovative, first-of-its-kind management style was succeeding. As a shepherd who cared deeply for his flock's welfare, or like a captain/provider, Moses had pioneered what is today called "servant leadership," a philosophy that dictates the leader exists to serve the people, not the people to serve the leader. Those who research organizational dynamics refer to it as "inverting the power pyramid." In fact, that is precisely what Moses intended to do. Armed with his insight from life in the palace, his training as a shepherd from Jethro, his brother as his wingman, the support of the Hebrew elders, a promise from the Lord to be there every step of the way, and his really cool shepherd's staff, Moses was prepared finally to challenge the very builder of pyramids to flip the power structure of Egypt and let his people go.

THE MOSAIC OF CHAPTER 2

1. True leaders are custodians or guardians of the hopes and dreams of those who they lead. A true leader's main focus should be empowering others to develop their strengths and talents for the good of the organization.
2. Moses was very "Millennial" in his approach to his "career," expressing a willingness to choose meaningful work over the proscribed models of success in the palace.
3. Midrash is a Hebrew word derived from the verb meaning "to enquire" or "to seek out," and it is both the name of the process and the most famous, oldest book of Jewish commentary on the Torah.
4. The Talmud is a book of Jewish instruction and rabbinical scholarship that roughly equates in function to the Islamic Hadith.
5. The depth of Moses' humility was known only to God. Moses needed a burning bush experience to see himself as God did.
6. For various reasons, Moses instinctively knew his limitations and insisted on help.
7. The Moses narrative is the oldest known example of "servant leadership," a philosophy that defies easy categorization, but it is most closely associated with a participative style of management.

3

A Ruthless Overbearing Tyrant versus a Humble Servant Leader

Anybody who has ever held a job knows that not all managers are good leaders and not all good leaders are decent managers. Some people are gifted at supervising select aspects of a business but not so much when it comes to inspiring people or leading an entire company. Conversely, many effective leaders have the needed "big picture" skills or the dynamic personality to galvanize disparate interests but lack the granular understanding of how the "day-to-day" gets done, so they need good managers along the chain of command. In the perfect work-world, the best leaders are also the best managers. They are legends.

Unfortunately, of course, this is rare. Too often, owing to the "right" pedigree, powerful connections, some personal success, or even just a persuasive image created by a well-written CV, many people with limited interpersonal charm and management chops end up in important leadership positions. This situation usually negatively impacts the very employees these loser-leaders should be helping to succeed. Hallways can be harrowing places when an ill-suited man or woman is in a place of authority and interfering with the proper management of a corporate body. Not surprisingly, perhaps, the higher the position, the harder some poor leaders will fight to prolong their power trip. Research indicates that the less effective the leader, the more likely those men and women are to bury themselves in like a tick.

Katherine Crowley and Kathi Elster are business consultants who specialize in office power dynamics and coauthors of three books that explore methods of surviving bad bosses in the workplace: *Working with You Is Killing Me: Freeing Yourself from Emotional Traps at Work*; *Working for You Isn't Working for Me: How to Get Ahead When Your Boss Holds You Back*; and *Mean Girls at Work: How to Stay Professional When Things Get Personal*. Among their findings, Crowley and Elster were able to establish consistent archetypes that ranged from "difficult bosses" to "extreme bosses." The researchers contend that toxic leadership varies in style, though all share common root causes based in fear, self-preservation at the expense of the organization, and lack of empathy for the chaos they cause. To those just entering the workforce or merely trying to succeed despite obstacles, thousands of self-help books such as these provide cogent advice to millions of people worldwide.

Yet, it should go without saying, as Moses and Aaron were traveling to put Pharaoh on notice that the God of the Hebrews was demanding the release of the enslaved, there were no self-help business books lying around in the desert to guide them through the negotiations. Still, who needs a self-help book when you're on a mission from God? Just ask the Blues Brothers. As instructed, Moses and Aaron led off with God's request that the Israelites get some bonding time away from the whip.

Joined by the appointed leaders of Israelites and following God's script, then, Moses and Aaron pressed their case to Pharaoh: God commands you to allow the half-million Jews to have what we might think of today as a "spiritual retreat" or a convocation in the desert to renew their faith. "This is what the Lord, the God of Israel, says," Moses explained, "'Let my people go, so that they may hold a festival to me in the wilderness.'"

And just as God predicted, Pharaoh treated Moses and Aaron like out-of-town labor organizers attempting to unionize local coal miners. "Who is the Lord, that I should obey him and let Israel go?" Pharaoh scoffed. "I do not know the Lord, and I will not let Israel go." At this point, the Hebrew elders chimed in to confirm with whom Pharaoh was trifling. "The God of the Hebrews has met with us," they said. "Now, let us take a three-day journey into the wilderness to offer sacrifices to the Lord our God, or he may strike us with plagues or with the sword."

Although God had previously stated that Pharaoh was in the divine crosshairs for his arrogance and cruelty to the Israelites, in this verse, the elders indicate that *they* are afraid of divine retribution, too. Remember, they were on board with Moses and Aaron after Moses showed them the whole staff-snake-staff thing; they witnessed firsthand Moses' divine bona fides. In modern sales parlance, this request might be categorized as a "value proposition" to Pharaoh: Allowing the slaves to have a camp revival meeting in the desert could raise worker morale and increase productivity. All Pharaoh had to do was let them have a couple of days off, and maybe nobody had to get hurt.

In the Qur'an, although the Hebrew elders do not rate an appearance by name, there is nothing in the text to suggest that they weren't there. For that matter, in the Muslim tradition, even though Moses had asked God to make Aaron his companion, Aaron does nothing in front of Pharaoh except be Moses' wingman. The Qur'an acknowledges Moses' concern that Aaron does the talking because "He is more eloquent in speech than I" (Al Qasas-28:34), but the rest of the narrative does not reflect that. Indeed, a silent Aaron standing near Moses is the way the confrontation is usually depicted in the movies.

To stress that point even further, in the Qur'an, the nature of Moses' confrontation of Pharaoh is noticeably, dramatically snappier. According to Ibn Kathir's summation in *The Stories of the Prophets*, despite all of Moses' protestations that he does not speak well or may have a speech impairment of some sort, the exchange between Moses and Pharaoh in the Qur'an reads like dialogue from an Aaron Sorkin script:

> Pharaoh listened to Moses' speech with disdain. He thought that Moses was crazy because he dared to question his supreme position. Then he raised his hand and asked: "What do you want?"
>
> Moses answered: "I want you to send the children of Israel with us."

Pharaoh asked: "Why should I send them, as they are my slaves?"

Moses replied: "They are the slaves of Allah, Lord of the Worlds."

Pharaoh then inquired sarcastically if his name was Moses. Moses said "Yes."

"Are you not the Moses whom we picked up from the Nile as a helpless baby? Are you not the Moses whom we reared in this palace, who ate and drank from our provisions and whom our wealth showered with charity? Are you not the Moses who is a fugitive, the killer of an Egyptian man, if my memory does not betray me? It is said that killing is an act of disbelief. Therefore, you were a disbeliever when you killed. You are a fugitive from justice and you come to speak to me! What were you talking about Moses, I forgot?"

Zing. At this point in the negotiation—by all outward appearances, anyway—Pharaoh is owning Moses like, well, a boss. In fact, nothing that Pharaoh says is false: From birth, Moses enjoyed the benefits of the very system he is now challenging. Moses prospered while his people suffered; he killed a man in an act of rage—accidental or not—and did not become a true believer in the faith of his birth until he escaped to the desert. Although presumably the death warrant against him from Pharaoh's father has expired, Moses is still a fugitive from justice when he comes to accuse Pharaoh Jr. himself of injustice to the Jews.

Pharaoh's tactic was intentional. Pharaoh's use of Moses' incriminating history deflects from Pharaoh's own much larger crimes. Employing sarcasm, keeping Moses on the defensive, and then later using a menacing, threatening tone with which he lashes Moses, Ibn Kathir states, "Pharaoh deliberately adopted the style of the absolute ruler." As long as there have been human bosses, there have been human tyrants, but the operative word there is "human." Pharaoh still had to pee.

This is more than a vulgarism; it's an important theological point regarding the humanity of those venerated in our holiest histories. The temptation of the modern reader of any tradition's scriptures—Jewish, Christian, or Muslim—might be to imagine that 5,000 years ago, human beings were composed physically, mentally, and spiritually of some non-human divine substance. The proof that human beings of the biblical era and today are the same, however, is in the continued relevance of the holy scriptures themselves: We see ourselves in the humanness of the men and women of the Bible and the Qur'an because they are as flawed and frail as we are in equal measure—and we would be just as recognizable to them.

This is because all evidence indicates human beings have always been lusty, gluttonous, greedy, slothful, and given to anger, envy, and pride, to name a few characteristics. If this were not true, there never would have been a need for religious scriptures that pushed our ancestors beyond their baser instincts just as they push us. Humanity's pursuit of virtuous behavior is as old as human weakness itself. For example, whenever group success is understood as more assured than survival on one's own, sages of all religions have underscored the importance of strong community bonds. Different wordings of "love your neighbors as yourselves" found in almost every faith's holy writings over thousands of years and thousands of miles apart might be the best evidence that humans are basically the same everywhere—and we have not evolved that much.

Though Pharaoh's legend looms large over many millennia and three religious traditions, ultimately, Pharaoh is just as flesh and blood as any petty tyrant in the news today—and maybe not even as bad. According to office dynamic researchers Crowley and Elster, in fact, there always have been many pharaohs big and small in business and government and still are. In Crowley and Elster's opinion, "Approaching the Pharaoh from the perspective of boss profiles, he would qualify for *two kinds* of extreme bosses: (1) the Persecutor; (2) the Controlling Egomaniac." There, in the overlap between those two leaders-from-hell archetypes, Pharaoh was formidable, but he was not otherworldly. Crowley and Elster know well because they encounter bosses who are Persecutors and Controlling Egomaniacs all the time but not always combined.

"Persecuting bosses are those individuals who target a certain person or group of people, and set out to make their lives miserable. They see the targeted population as threatening, and seek to squelch them—mentally, psychologically, and physically—in any way that they can." For example, Jews had been invited to relocate to Egypt and prospered under many generations of benevolent kings; however, by the time that Pharaoh's father took the throne, the Children of Israel had been scapegoated and enslaved as potential enemies of the state just based on their customs and beliefs.

But there was more to the depth of Pharaoh's deceptions, per Crowley and Elster: "Controlling egomaniac bosses are those managers who command respect by virtue of their authority and accomplishments, but also insist on controlling every aspect of their organization. These bosses are charming when they need to be, but overall ruthless when it comes to maintaining their power and control."

This meant that the Egyptian population was the beneficiary of a murderous, egomaniacal despot such as Pharaoh. If the average Egyptian were willing to think too critically, Pharaoh might seem like a caring, detail-oriented king who was committed to keeping the country safe from invaders in all forms. For Hebrew slaves, however, Pharaoh's management style meant being stigmatized and abused as a suspicious "other," a threat to the Egyptian way of life despite having lived there peacefully for hundreds of years. In an effort to exploit these marginalized laborers to his satisfaction, Pharaoh—like all persecuting bosses—was never above lying or manipulating popular opinion to get his way. Through propaganda and fear-mongering, talented and charming persecuting bosses such as Pharaoh seem to know intuitively how to inflame certain publics into perceiving "the other" in their midst as scorn-worthy, second-class citizens.

This parallels the white nationalists in America who relish President Trump's use of the word "invaders" to describe brown-skinned, would-be immigrants and refugees coming to the US southern border—or, for that matter, the white nationalists of 1920s Germany who were so inspired by Adolf Hitler's conspiratorial rhetoric regarding German Jews. Even though ninth-century Emperor Charlemagne had invited

Jews into Germany for economic reasons, Jewish assimilation was not 100 percent complete. Just as in Pharaonic Egypt, Jews still observed their own customs, family traditions, and dress and religious practices. By 1925, however, while serving time in jail for high treason, Hitler, an Austrian-born World War I veteran who had served as a German army corporal, wrote a book targeting Jews as "the other" that was even more devastating than anything imagined in Pharaoh's Egypt.

In *Mein Kampf*, Hitler not only blamed the Jews for Germany's defeat in World War I but also made a case for their global annihilation. Before he was crushed by the Allies in World War II, Hitler, his henchmen, and a complicit populace conspired to mass murder more than six million Jews (some say more than seven million) through a network of Nazi work/death camps. Against the backdrop of the horror of the gas chambers, it is easy to see why Oskar Schindler, a German factory owner who shielded 1,200 Jews from certain death by cajoling, bribing, and fooling Nazi party officials, is honored as a modern, small-scale, Moses-type leader willing to risk his own life to serve others.

Another epic Pharaoh figure who falls under Crowley and Elster's persecutor/egomaniac extreme-boss model was Idi Amin, the president of Uganda between 1971 and 1979. Born in northwestern Uganda while it was under British colonial rule to parents who separated after his birth, Amin received only rudimentary education. He joined the British colonial army, and after his country gained independence from the United Kingdom, he rose ruthlessly through the ranks until he became commander of the army in Uganda. Anticipating that corruption and cruelty charges were about to be brought against him by the popularly elected Ugandan government and its president, Amin conspired with the country's prime minister to overthrow the president. When the smoke cleared, Amin declared himself president of Uganda and began to systematically eliminate all opposition, including those who had helped him achieve power.

For almost an entire decade thereafter, Amin's name was synonymous with despotic cruelty. After overseeing the mass executions of Ugandan tribes who had expressed loyalty to others, Amin terrorized his own people through a brutal, corrupt government fortified by loyal security forces who exerted draconian control over all aspects of Ugandan life. Amin's persecution of Asians living in Uganda—targeting them as Pharaoh targeted Jews—led to their eventual expulsion from the country. This development, in turn, brought about the collapse of the Ugandan economy, which drove the people into further misery and resulted in increased secret police abuses.

Once the tragic truth about Amin's murderous excesses was exposed internationally, Amin became known as the "Butcher of Uganda." Before he could be stopped, Amin persecuted, imprisoned, or killed as many as half a million people during his reign of terror while giving himself lofty, narcissistic titles such as "His Excellency, President for Life," "Lord of All the Beasts of the Earth," and—to everybody's dismay—the "King of Scotland." This is consistent with Crowley and Elster's research, which indicates controlling, egomaniacal, persecuting bosses maintain sympathetic views of themselves despite the heartless, manipulative acts of cruelty on display to everybody else.

The same thing happens in the Moses narrative. For example, in response to entreaties that Pharaoh fear the God of the Israelites and allow the slaves time to celebrate God in the wilderness, the Qur'an adds Pharaoh's umbrage that Moses did not consider *him* a god: "After declaring his divinity, Pharaoh asked Moses how he dared to worship another god. The punishment for this crime was imprisonment. It was not permitted for anyone to worship anyone other than the Pharaoh. Moses understood that the intellectual arguments did not succeed." Indeed, it is impossible to reason with tyrannical bosses because they are incapable of compromise and intolerant of dissent.

So, instead of honoring the request from his "employees" for some rest, Pharaoh doubled the slaves' workload. Pharaoh first tried to drive a wedge between Team Moses and the Israelite elders by saying, "Moses and Aaron, why you are taking the people away from their labor. . . . You are stopping them from working!" After ordering the slaves back to work, Pharaoh commanded the Egyptian slave drivers and the Hebrew overseers under them to no longer supply the people with the straw necessary to make quality bricks. This act was intended to be a major hardship, as fulfilling the king's construction agenda required tons of bricks to be handmade from a mixture of the rich Nile-basin mud (which was heavy in clay) and straw.

The mud-and-straw-into-brick formula is a simple one, even to this day: After mixing together water, mud (clay), and straw, thoroughly knead the ingredients, and then press a clump of the recipe into a brick-shaped mold. Letting the contents sit until the mixture has firmed enough to remove the mold, place the still moist brick on the ground to dry in the sun. As the fibrous straw absorbs the water, dries, and breaks down, it acts as a binder by creating a natural rebar as the bricks solidify.

Handmaking bricks was dirty, labor-intensive work, and each slave was required to produce a certain number each day or be punished—and that's with the straw being provided. Forcing the slaves to retrieve their own straw, scrounge for chaff, or risk making brittle bricks that might not be strong enough to pass inspection—all the while maintaining the same brick quota—was not a sustainable business plan. In short, as the old, trite slogan on the wall sign goes, "The beatings will continue until morale improves." Pharaoh's abuse both taunted Moses and punished the slaves for stepping out of line, for sure, but it was also a game of diminishing returns for Pharaoh's own construction goals. No matter how hard the slave drivers beat the Israelites, production did not improve. When the Hebrew overseers appealed to Pharaoh to allow them to go to the wilderness and worship, the king said, "Lazy, that's what you are—lazy! That is why you keep saying, 'Let us go and sacrifice to the Lord!' Now, get to work."

Pharaoh's scheme to get the Hebrew elders to turn on Moses and Aaron for intervening on their behalf worked, at least in part. The Bible says, "When they left Pharaoh, they found Moses and Aaron waiting to meet them, and they said, 'May the Lord look on you and judge you! You have made us obnoxious to Pharaoh and his officials and have put a sword in their hand to kill us.'" So it often goes with change-agents who are pitted against institutional resistance; it's bleakest before the breakthrough. The Children of Israel had been praying that God would end their misery. God heard their cries and sent Moses. Now they were crying because it was going to be hard. Change usually is.

In the Christian tradition, Jesus' disciples follow a similar pattern many times. First of all, in an echo of the Twelve Tribes of Israel (again, the twelve sons of Jacob, whom God had renamed "Israel," who had migrated to Egypt centuries earlier), the followers closest to Jesus, known collectively as the apostles ("messengers" from the Greek), also numbered twelve. The apostles witnessed amazing acts of Jesus that were every bit as miraculous as a wooden staff turned into a snake and then back again; yet they, too, could become fearful and cower before human, earthly authority.

Just like the Hebrew elders of Egypt who hours earlier had been sharing their witness of God's strength with Pharaoh, according to the Christian story, Jesus' inner circle seemed to suffer from spontaneous amnesia and had to be "retaught" by Jesus many times in their travels. Famously, the apostle named Simon, who was renamed Peter ("rock" from the Greek), the one whom Jesus predicted would be "the rock upon which I will build my church," denied knowing Jesus at three separate times on the night of Jesus' arrest. Had Peter lost his faith, or just his nerve?

Faith can be as steady as a rock, but a wave of doubt can be as subversive as rushing waters that can dislodge the largest stones by eroding the undergirding earth. The rock of faith itself may never change, but it can wobble on loose soil. This can be true of any plan. Entire multinational corporations have been known to conduct research on their goods and services, develop an action plan that requires a change of approach to ensure the longevity of the company's success, strategically implement the plan, and then abandon those goals at the slightest pushback from consumers. Many people have faith, but they lack resilience in the face of adversity.

Resilience—the ability to recover from misfortune, to stay a course mentally, to physically go the distance by resisting the natural, human inclination to retreat—might be as (or more!) important than faith itself, especially when facing down seemingly impossible odds with no timeline apparent. Many people have faith who still eventually "tap out" when the going gets tough. Another way to look at the confluence of faith and resilience is that the faith Moses and Aaron had was more than just another noun; it had become a verb.

Exploring the difference between faith as a noun and "to faith" as a verb is controversial to some. Christian theologians dispute the significance between the Greek noun for faith, transliterated into English as *pistos*, and the Greek verb based on the same word root that is most often associated with the English verb "to believe": *pisteuo*. The debate will not be settled in this book, either, but an alternate translation of *pisteuo* relates to a verb with no English equivalent: "to faith." "To be faithing" does not make sense in English. Faith, as any noun, is something that one can have, or not have, like a boat or a hat. The Bible and the Qur'an are replete with stories of men and women who had faith, lost it, and gained it back again.

But just as there is a difference between being on a diet and dieting, having a faith and faithing reflect different experiences. Anybody can say they have a diet plan that they stop or start, but fewer people incorporate their diet plan into a continuous course of action toward a greater goal. Faithing implies faith in action, or faith achieved through action. Unfortunately, the closest English verb in usage to faithing is "believing," which is how the verb is usually translated into English.

For example, when the apostles of Jesus risked certain death at the hands of their Roman overlords by going from town to town comforting the afflicted and healing the sick, they were faithing, an experience well beyond "believing." After Jesus' crucifixion, after Peter surrendered to the servanthood to which he had been called regardless of the consequences for his safety, he finally did become the rock on which Jesus would build his church. For Muslims, once more, the elevation of faith from a noun to a verb parallels the use of the Arabic word "Islam": to submit or surrender.

Jewish, Christian, or Muslim—everybody knows somebody who has a noun-faith. Perhaps most people do. In the media, every day, we see showy people who wave their faith around as if it were a flashy, personal accessory. Politicians, celebrities, and talking heads often posture themselves using the language of religious commitment, but they are less interested in self-sacrifice than they are in getting reelected, publicizing a new media project, or promoting a political agenda. In contrast to the unsung men and women who effortlessly blend leadership with servanthood in their daily faithing, sometimes it seems as if the majority of people we see on screens—both large and small—simply turn their faith on and off as easily as a video camera, submitting only to the service of their egos, ultimately uninterested in surrendering themselves in the process.

Malcolm X might have started off as somebody who was dying to be famous, but in the end, he died faithing. Born Malcolm Little, the son of a Baptist minister and a homemaker wife, Malcolm grew up in relative prosperity and stability despite having his family uprooted from house and home twice by racial threats and attacks. X did well in his desegregated school until one day when his teacher asked him what he wanted to become when he grew up. X said he wanted to become a lawyer. The teacher told X that he could not become a lawyer but maybe a carpenter. That was the end of X's dream and the start of the unraveling of his life. Dejected, he dropped out, took up odd jobs, and fell into bad company.

Drugs and theft led to his incarceration. As a lost soul, X found comfort and purpose in the teachings of visitors from the Nation of Islam, a group that combined elements of Islam with black nationalism. After converting to the Islam practiced by "the Nation," X immersed himself in reading and debating. When he was released, he was a self-educated, inspirational orator who advocated a total separation of the races.

At the end of a tour of Africa, however, X went to Mecca to perform the rituals of the hajj, a trip that resulted in his rejection of the Nation of Islam and his conversion to orthodox Sunni Islam. For the first time in his life, during the hajj, X witnessed the mixing of people from various races being considerate and brotherly toward one another in a huge, swirling mass of humanity.

X's rejection of the Nation of Islam earned him their enmity. Despite courageous efforts to gain respect and rights for all black Americans, X was murdered on stage while addressing a large crowd of his admirers. Like Moses, X was born among the oppressed and marginalized people of his time but also raised in a comfortable home and school environment. Somewhat akin to Moses accidentally killing a man and having to run away to escape incarceration, X spent many years lost in a spiritual wilderness before he was found. Moses was charged by God with liberating the Hebrew slaves; Malcolm X was called to liberate the descendants of African slaves still living in social and economic bondage.

Each life also ended with goals in sight but out of reach. Moses died before crossing into the Promised Land. X was killed before he saw any tangible improvement from the 1964 Civil Rights Act. Yet both left a legacy that started with their submission to servanthood.

The same could be said for Theodor Herzl, a Viennese journalist known in modern Israel as Hozeh Ha'Medinah, or "the Visionary of the State." Like Moses, Herzl was not born in the Holy Land, but rather in Austria, where anti-Semitism was as institutionalized as racism was in Malcolm X's America.

In his book *Der Judenstaadt* (*The Jewish State*) in 1896, Herzl advocated the return of the Jews to a safe homeland in Palestine. Like Moses' confrontation of Pharaoh, Herzl pleaded his case to the rulers of Europe and, in particular, to the Turkish sultan who ruled the Near East, and he asked for their help in establishing a Jewish state in the ancestral Land of Israel. Unlike Moses, though, who started his career at age eighty and spent the next forty years taking the Hebrew slaves out of Egypt, leading them through the desert, giving the world the Ten Commandments at Mount Sinai, and bringing them to the gates of the Promised Land, Herzl died suddenly in 1904 at age forty-four. Submission to the service of others is no guarantee of a long life.

Asher Ginsberg, writing under the pen name Ahad Ha'am ("one of the people"), was a preeminent thinker of Cultural Zionism when Theodor Herzl founded what is known as Political Zionism. Ginsberg was a notable essayist, and one of his most widely read works was titled "Moses," in which he sought to answer the question of whether Moses actually existed.

As Ahad Ha'am, he argues against searching for the historical Moses. He weighs the historicity of Moses against the significance of Moses as history's premiere prophet, whose impact on the Jewish people and on human civilization is unmatched. Did Moses actually exist? Ahad Ha'am's answer is that Moses exists spiritually in every generation and continues to guide his people to this day. The celebration of the exodus from Egypt observed by Jews every year on Passover is one of the foundations of the Jewish faith and of monotheism. One cannot conceive of a Jewish people or of monotheism without a Moses.

In fact, although Muslim scholars generally accept the biblical 120-year lifespan of Moses, the Qur'an itself makes no mention of the age of Moses or Aaron at any stage of their story arcs. There is also no clear indication that the age of any prophet or divine messenger had any relationship at all to his or her accomplishments. While some messengers lived long, Jesus and Muhammed did not, the latter having received his calling at the age of forty and dying at the age of sixty-two. A divine call to servant leadership is never limited by human chronology, only willingness. If the reader could picture it, an online ad that reads, "Help Wanted: Men and women with the ability to put their faith in a cause that helps others and the requisite resilience to see it through," is displayed on some divine job site right now.

Perhaps there is no age restriction on service because, human nature being what it is, the struggle between self-interested oppressors and selfless liberators is eternal. Crowley and Elster warn that persecuting, egomaniacal bosses are difficult to beat at their own game; our holy scriptures assure us that all things come together for good for those who work for a higher purpose. The battle lines are drawn thusly: Those who sacrifice their personal and/or financial success for the betterment of others may never see the Land of Milk and Honey themselves. But theirs will be the profound satisfaction that comes from being a transformational leader, an effective change-agent, one who inspires those whom they serve to pursue a better vision for themselves and the world.

If the respect that comes from being a positively impactful Moses on your own turf inspires you even though it may not make you as rich as Pharaoh, read on. There is much work to do, but it may take a miracle or two before you are finished.

THE MOSAIC OF CHAPTER 3

1. Not all managers are good leaders, and not all good leaders are decent managers; petty tyrants end up in leadership positions in organizations big and small.
2. All evidence indicates human beings have always been lusty, gluttonous, greedy, slothful, and given to anger, envy, and pride, to name a few characteristics.
3. If this were not true, there never would have been a need for religious scriptures that pushed our ancestors beyond their baser instincts just as they push us.
4. Pharaoh and Moses were just men of their time; the struggle between self-interested oppressors and selfless liberators is eternal.
5. Do you have a noun-faith or faith like a verb?
6. Resilience is as important to people of faith as faith itself.
7. There always have been pharaohs big and small in business and government and still are.

4

Moses and the "Miracle" of Humble Leadership

As mentioned in chapter 2, because a miracle does not require a violation of the laws of physics, it can be said that millions of miracles happen every day, all over the world. They do not have to be big events, either. Miracles belong in a realm that is merely beyond human understanding, something that is "a little wondrous to see." For some, the splendor of nature—such as an amazing sunset—could be viewed as a miracle; nothing is more miraculous than the birth of a healthy baby. More specifically, in the Judeo-Christian tradition, one can choose to believe in miracles or not, but one cannot explain them scientifically. A miracle cannot be measured or quantified; it simply "is." Griffin, a time-traveling alien in *Men in Black 3*, put it this way: "A miracle is what seems impossible but happens anyway." A story from the Ukraine that made the rounds on the internet might be a good example of this concept.

An emaciated stray dog with beautiful blue eyes was rescued from certain death on the Ukrainian streets and brought to a local animal shelter for care. The volunteers fed him and treated his wounds while they posted a photo and a standard notification of his availability for adoption online. Although the message had been intended to inspire potential dog parents, the notice got traction in Ukrainian social media. A few days later, the shelter got a call from a nearby woman who wondered whether this dog could be her own pup who had been missing for two years.

When she came to the shelter to determine whether the dog was hers, their reunion was captured on smartphone video. Standing on his hind legs, the large dog was embraced by the woman as if he were her Prodigal Son; she cried as the dog smothered her with slobbery kisses. The unlikeliness of the whole chain of events—the dog's rescue, the shared posting, the slim chance that the missing dog's true owner even would see the photo or further recognize him as a grown dog, and then the demonstrable celebration of both the dog and the woman on seeing each other after all this time apart—moved the shelter volunteers, who called it a "miracle reunion" on their Facebook page. And they were right.

Thousands of miles away in the United States, another miracle was in the offing. In a medium-sized, trendy advertising company, a creative, experienced woman in her fifties with a reputation for teamwork and expediency had been brought on to save an important, cash-flowing project for a key client. For the purposes of her use here, the name "Amy" and other details of her situation have been changed.

Amy's arrival was seen as a positive sign that the agency was committed to preserving a neglected project that had been suffering at the hands of a previous content creator who had run afoul of the company's corporate practices. Because advertising media work is often a younger person's game, and Amy was much older than many of her colleagues, she was grateful for a new opportunity to show what she could do and was emboldened by the confidence that had been placed in her to see the project through. Still, she could not help but notice many people were "retiring" or moving on just as she got there, and she wondered whether there was an underlying problem she had not figured out yet.

Not surprising in light of her track record, due to Amy's hard work, long hours, and talent as a leader, the project was saved. The campaign was then nominated for awards through a prestigious, national industrial competition, and she was offered new challenges within the company that were consistent with her capabilities. For a brief period of time, she was celebrated as a hero.

But then hallway whispers began to undermine Amy's status and her professional progress. Her previously collegial relationship with the two women just below the general-manager level who brought her in suddenly went cold. Even though she was hired to be a producer of creative content, she noticed that all of her suggestions about new projects or new ways to look at old projects were being shot down or sidetracked. Despite her previous success, the women to whom she answered started giving her menial assignments that typically would have been given to a less seasoned content creator or even to a freelancer. When she expressed incredulity, she was reminded that her employee agreement said that she had to work on any project given to her. Surprised by the sudden change of tone, Amy felt she was being stifled.

Her new colleagues expressed to her that management was averse to change. Although a few times a year they held a large staff meeting and claimed to be open to all input, the reality was that every idea presented was cynically shot down as not good or too expensive. Amy appeared to be only the latest example of somebody targeted by the two women just below the top for being a threat to the status quo.

Furthermore, these managers—who thrived by covering for each other to the owner—hired people who they thought were controllable. The consensus theory appeared to be that Amy was expected to be more deferential and compliant because she was older than the average hire. Leaders who are unsure of themselves often recruit teammates who are less qualified than themselves to avoid being challenged in areas of their own weaknesses. Effective leaders, however, are confident in themselves and focus their efforts on accomplishing the mission. Hence, they seek people who will complement them in areas where they perceive themselves to be weak or lacking. Moses asked for someone he knew to be capable, his own brother Aaron, for specific reasons, not mere familiarity or favor.

Because Amy was clearly more competent than her managers might have suspected, the whisper campaign started characterizing her as "rogue," not a team player, somebody who was only interested in personal glory. While her two female superiors were joined together in casting Amy as a renegade employee who needed to be controlled and corrected at all times, over time, it became evident that the subtle campaign against her was being coordinated actively by only one of the women—"Gayle"—one of the longest-running employees in the company.

Meanwhile, agency colleagues continued reaching out to Amy discreetly to reaffirm to her that she had done nothing wrong and to hang in there. Although she was still relatively new, behind closed doors, Amy was warned that the two women above her had a pretty good thing going. They never had to work long hours, their salaries were ample, and they appeared to be on cruise control to retirement. To the owner, they always could say, "We keep asking for new ideas, but nobody has come up with a winner yet." On paper, it appeared as though they were trying. Others in the company later expressed concern when negative comments about Amy—often delivered by Gayle with a smile or a tone of "we're here to help you!"—became the norm in weekly staff meetings in front of everybody.

To make matters worse, a younger female freelancer with less experience was hired by Gayle to "help oversee" Amy's work, an unnecessary complication both women found confusing. Some colleagues saw it as an unforgivable insult geared to make the more resilient worker quit or fail. Because some previous employees had decided it was easier to leave the company rather than to endure the strain of surviving similar palace intrigue, Amy was convinced that she would not last and began to prepare her resume. Even though Amy considered herself tougher than that, a few afternoons even required a tearful call to friends behind closed doors for emotional support. Her colleagues kept encouraging her to fight, but as the days went by, she could feel herself trying to hold it together just to get through work. Amy felt powerless. It would take a miracle to turn the situation around.

Jewish tradition dating back to post-biblical times makes it clear that all miracles transcend human action. Also, one should not rely on a miracle either from God or from other humans. In other words, if a miracle is meant to happen, it will, but it cannot be ordered or counted on. Ordering up a miracle through petition prayers, for example, is commonly called "God-as-valet" theology, and it puts God on our own willful timeline instead of us agreeing to live on God's.

From a strictly Islamic perspective, just because we do not understand why what happened happened, the happening does not yield a true miracle. A combination of trickery and mesmerizing may cause one to see what is *not there* or not see *what is there*. A chance combination of pharmaceuticals administered in an unplanned manner may suddenly cure an illness. A slight turn of events may save a person from being hit by a boulder. All of these are extraordinary events that ordinarily pass for miracles but are merely happenstance.

For example, there is Pharaoh's response to Moses' miracle rod. After God once more produced a snake out of Moses' staff, the Bible states, "Pharaoh also called for the wise men and sorcerers, and they—along with the Egyptian magicians—did the same thing with their secret arts. So each one threw down his staff, and it became a serpent." In the Qur'an, it says that even Moses himself feared the false snakes—momentarily. But the rods of Pharaoh's magicians only became snakes in the eye of the beholders. It was trickery, the Qur'an implies, but because Pharaoh's magicians were masters of their craft, and Moses had no training in magic, the humble prophet suddenly felt outmatched. However, God reassured Moses that he was not alone.

Then God instructed Moses to throw down his rod again, and this time the rod became a serpent that gobbled up all of the magicians' false snakes. In the Bible, of course, it is a little different. In Exodus, God commands Aaron to throw down the staff that turns into a snake that then snarfs up the magicians' illusions. This key difference goes back to the narrative split over whether Moses or his brother Aaron was doing all the talking. The Qur'an identifies the importance of Aaron's helpful presence, but Moses speaks. In the Bible, because Moses is the prophet and not his brother, God tells Moses what to say, Moses tells Aaron, and Aaron proclaims it to all who would listen. The end result is the same, however. The turning of the rod into a serpent was not a human achievement but a power beyond Moses and Aaron—and beyond Pharaoh's magicians as well. It was God who intervened.

In that intervention lies the true nature of miracles and its relation to faith. From the Islamic point of view, a miracle happens when God changes the normal course of human events, which is to be expected. There is nothing more complicated than that; God can do anything by simply saying, "Be . . . and it is." To satisfy the question "What is a true miracle?" in Islam, the best answer is "A faith in a power beyond human imagination." Our path to true understanding is what is the most miraculous thing because we have transcended our own limited human thinking.

As an illustration of that idea, in the chapter named "Ascension" ('isra), the Qur'an recounts how God took the prophet Muhammed from his home in Makkah (Mecca) to the mosque in Jerusalem and then caused him to ascend to the heavens before bringing him back to his home. In human time, this all happened within moments. Even the greatest prophet would not be capable of doing this on his or her own.

When Muhammed spoke of this amazing journey, some of the nonbelievers went to Abu Bakar, the prophet's close companion/father-in-law, and sneered that Muhammed was now telling strange tales. This couldn't have happened, they claimed. Abu Bakar asked, "Did the Messenger of God really say that?" "Yes, he did," replied the nonbelievers. "Then this must be true, because the Messenger of God does not lie." After this response, Abu Bakar came to be known as Abu Bakar Siddiq, or "Abu Bakar the truthful."

Another example of a true miracle in Islam is the Qur'an itself. The Arab tribes among whom Muhammed lived were highly skilled in language arts and especially appreciated for their beautiful poetry. However, the revelations of the Qur'an, it is believed, far surpassed what the Arabs of the time were capable of producing and, in fact, created its own inimitable language. Not just the prophetic messages but the actual Qur'an itself challenged the best Arab poets to produce one verse that could compete with the exquisite quality of the Qur'an. The tribal poets failed because the Qur'an was God's own words—a divine intervention, a miraculous book about miracles.

In the Judeo-Christian tradition, the first translation of the Hebrew Bible into Greek has a similar reputation. By the third century BCE, Hebrew was no longer spoken commonly because Greek had become the *lingua franca* of the Middle East. Motivated by his interest in scholarship, Ptolemy II Philadelphus, the son of one of Alexander the Great's generals, ordered a new translation of the Bible from Hebrew into Greek so that it could be more widely enjoyed. Though he was not Jewish, Ptolemy II was raised with the Grecian belief that venerated ancient wisdom. In keeping with Ptolemy II's order, more or less seventy of the greatest scholars took more or less seventy days in isolation from each other to translate the Hebrew Bible into Greek. When the seventy scholars were finished, the separate texts were compared, and, according to the legend, not one word of difference could be found between them. Hence, the early Greek translation of the Old Testament part of the Bible is still referred to as the Septuagint, meaning "seventy" in Greek, which, in biblical numerology, implies "divine completeness."

Historians dispute the entire matter, of course, and modern biblical scholarship has corrected many scribal errors in the Septuagint, but perhaps these stories survive for the simple reason that humans benefit by even considering the seemingly impossible. The Qur'an's chapter titled "Kahf" relates the story of a few young people who chose to steer away from an unbelieving society and lay down in a cave. They lay there for a number of years, after which they woke up and thought they had slept for only a few days. God states that he had kept them alive all these years because they were God-fearing souls who had turned away from a godless society. Is it out-and-out crazy, or another illustration of "A faith in a power beyond human imagination"?

Some Christian theological traditions would agree that God determines every event, big or small, miraculous or mundane, a position completely consistent with the Islamic perspective that not even a leaf can fall from a tree without God's knowledge and God's permission. Perhaps this notion explains our human obsession with fall colors; even atheists have been known to refer to autumn as a "miracle of nature." If nothing else, this suggests that people generally like the idea of miracles even if they cannot agree on what they are.

For example, most modern readers fall into one of four categories: First, there are those who believe literally in God-centered miracles and do not question them. Second are those who do not believe in miracles in the "God says be . . . and it is" sense, instead seeing miracles as an allegory, which, in the case of the Ten Plagues, provides an example of God's unlimited power to force a tyrant to let his slaves go free. Third, we have those who look for scientific explanations, such as the water of the Nile turning red being the result of some sort of infestation. Finally, there are those who dismiss the whole concept as fictions that have no basis in fact or reality.

Charles Pellegrino is a successful author of science fiction and speculative science theory books who may be best known as the originator of the "Jurassic Park Recipe," which is Pellegrino's original published proposition that dinosaurs could be cloned from DNA extracted from amber-covered bloodsucking insects, which years later became the foundation for the *Jurassic Park* franchise. Pellegrino also contributed to Israeli-Canadian writer/director/producer Simcha Jacobovici's History Channel special, *The Exodus Decoded* (2007).

As a knowledge seeker using the scientific model, Pellegrino identifies as an agnostic because he doubts everything while simultaneously admitting to a lack of certainty in his conclusions. "In my family, we respect other people's religions and do *not* (as do many American atheists) consider people of faith to be mentally ill," he says. "In fact, I sometimes envy the peace that some of my friends (many of them top-shelf scientists and explorers) find in their faith."

With regard to the famous Ten Plagues that Pharaoh brought down upon his own people every time he refused to let the Children of Israel go (in Exodus, the Nile turning to blood, an invasion of frogs, lice, wild animals or flies, the massive die-off of livestock, skin boils, storms of hail and fire, locusts, the loss of the sun, and death of the firstborns; there are only nine "signs" in the Qur'an, a few of them different), Pellegrino is one of the third type of readers who look for scientific explanations in the biblical accounts. From this point of view, the Ten Plagues of Exodus must have been related to a naturally occurring domino effect that began with volcanic explosions on the Greek island of Thera (also called Santorini) in the early 1600s BCE.

"We have clear evidence of a quarter-inch of volcanic dust, chemically finger-printable to the eruption of Thera/Santorini between 1628–1640 BCE, falling upon the Nile and its surroundings," Pellegrino asserts. "You could easily have seen this eruption—and the change in the Earth's albedo resulting thereof—from the surface of the moon and without the aid of binoculars." This catastrophic explosion on Thera was not that far from Egypt. "A quarter-inch of volcanic dust is enough to absolutely destroy crops. This event was sure to go down in both history and in myth. It was also squarely within the Eighteenth Dynasty's time of pharaohs."

Pellegrino's polymathic research often identifies possible intersections between archeology, history, religion, and physics. "Interestingly, for a while, monotheism takes root even in Egypt itself, during the Eighteenth Dynasty," Pellegrino says. "Thera/Santorini was the greatest volcanic upheaval civilization had ever seen so something quite dramatic must have occurred to cause such change, including apparent doubt in the 'old gods.' An eruption of such magnitude was bound to go down into the writings of future generations."

For believers who crave biblical-era archeological evidence that supports miraculous scriptural claims, the Thera/Santorini theory is a double-edged sword. Would scientific "proof" of various plagues in Egypt brought on by a volcanic eruption miles away substantiate or invalidate the miraculous timeline in Exodus? If the Ten Plagues really were compounding scientific repercussions from a volcano on the other side of the Mediterranean Sea, does that preclude the involvement of God? Couldn't the cascading aftereffects of a massive explosion still be viewed as the flick of a divine finger on the first domino of Pharaoh's downfall? For nonbelievers such as Pellegrino who struggle with the concept of divine intervention, perhaps even a scientific consideration of miracles would be the first step toward faith that, according to Islam, is the most miraculous thing there is? That is, even being open to miracles could be a miracle.

This brings us back to Amy, an experienced, professional content creator of no particular religious affiliation, who was suffering at the hands of Gayle, a pernicious office tyrant. This outwardly pleasant office fixture's main job was to oversee the budgets and resources used on campaigns. When Gayle was hired originally, it was in a different capacity, but slowly Gayle expanded her job in such a way that, eventually, everybody had to go through her to get anything done. Where there was a vacuum of power, she'd happily fill it. As she centralized her authority within the agency, Gayle was always smiling, always willing to help.

This situation meant Gayle had a powerful voice in deciding which projects got a green light. If Gayle was not involved in every phase of a new project, it would die of starvation. The open secret of getting Gayle on board was that she liked credit in the campaigns. Through office alliances, Gayle's name began to appear on the industry awards. Upper management didn't seem to notice (or mind) how powerful—or how petty—Gayle had become. The agency was running OK, and wasn't she always happy to help? Her whole life was the agency. However, some employees learned to fear what was behind the helpful smile.

By the time Amy reached out to authors/office dynamics consultants Katherine Crowley and Kathi Elster through a mutual friend, her situation had become intolerable. A public relations project in another division of Amy's company was being called a dumpster fire. The office gossip was that the PR project was going to crash and burn, and nobody wanted their name on it when it did. It was not just a hot potato—it was radioactive. The project was badly in need of fresh creativity and organizational skills. The owner of the agency had requested that some seasoned womanpower in Gayle's division be brought in to help turn it around. The project needed somebody with a reputation for teamwork and expediency who knew how to save a cash-flowing project for a key client.

When Gayle handed the file over to Amy with a big smile and ordered her to help the other division, she said the most curious thing: "Don't worry, it's not a punishment." *A punishment? Punishment for what?* Amy wondered. "No, it's *not* a punishment," Gayle reassured, as if that made more sense. Amy sensed a setup. When told about it later, Crowley agreed. Through their mutual friend, Crowley commiserated on what she had learned about the most difficult office tyrants over the years, and it wasn't good: "Sounds like a classic case of the Sacred Cow."

In Crowley and Elster's book *Working with You Is Killing Me*, the Sacred Cow extreme boss model is described as "those in positions of authority who've been promoted because of longevity, loyalty, personal connections, or family ties." Because of their perceived "tireless dedication to the company," few people suspect that the likable, usually sympathetic Sacred Cow boss has any other agenda than just giving until it hurts, but they do. Their greatest fear is being exposed as unqualified for the leadership position he or she has attained through default, so they constantly promote how much they sacrifice for the company.

"To avoid being found out," Crowley and Elster write, "the Sacred Cow does his or her best to maintain the existing systems—and coast." In the imagination of the Sacred Cow, change-agents are veritable wrecking balls. In the mind of the Sacred Cow, colleagues such as Amy must be controlled at all costs, but only in such a way that it will never blow back on them from above.

On the phone, Crowley described it this way: "Sacred Cows are so well protected within companies that there is no end-around. I'm sorry to say, the best way to deal with a Sacred Cow is to bow down to them."

One may feel blocked and trapped at every turn, but when it comes to Sacred Cows, the only person giving until it hurts will be the people around them. The more Amy should attempt to take on the Sacred Cow in a power struggle, Crowley warned, the more Amy would be cut out of key communications, isolated, and most likely fail.

"My best advice," Crowley offered, "is to back up and try to repair the relationship with Gayle, spend time working with her, and make her feel unthreatened." In this way, the Sacred Cow continues to succeed at the expense of others, but the pain of working with them is neutralized. Because of the pride Amy had in her work and in her ability to build effective teams, comforting and complimenting Gayle was going to be very difficult. Still, Amy promised to try to humble herself. Sadly, as unfair as she felt it was that she would have to be the one to leave, Amy also decided it was time to renew her search for another job.

The next three months were among the hardest of Amy's professional life. Every night, Amy vented her frustrations on walks with her husband, who encouraged her to be patient. "God never takes us halfway," Amy would later quote him as saying, "but that is sometimes hard to feel when you're in the middle of the desert." She went through with a couple of job interviews because talking to others made her feel a little less trapped, but nothing came of them.

After acknowledging her own limitations to change anybody else, Amy counted her many blessings, surrendered her ego, and did her best to let it be. She prayed, meditated, did yoga, and focused on the only thing over which she did have control: her own attitude toward Gayle. Instead of being resentful, as time went on, Amy learned to be sympathetic. *Something* must have made Gayle this way, Amy reasoned, and there was ample evidence that even if Gayle had once been able to control her inclination to sabotage innovation and progress at work, it had become an unconscious self-surviving reflex by now. Amy observed that Gayle was capable of occasionally apologizing when she had overstepped, but she was also apparently incapable of stopping.

Amy tried to be forgiving. In Judaism, each of us is obligated to for-give somebody who has wronged us if the offender asks with sincere contrition, but forgiveness can be offered regardless. According to Mus-lim tradition, the obligation on the faithful is to make seventy excuses for an offender's behavior—that is, resist assuming the worst possible motives and treat every infraction as a misunderstanding.

In Christianity, the story is told in the book of Matthew that the disci-ple Peter came to Jesus and asked, "Lord, how many times shall I forgive my brother who sins against me? Up to seven times?" Jesus answered, "I tell you, not just seven times, but seventy times seven." Since numbers in religious scriptures are often more symbolic than literal, the actual count does not matter as much as the edict: If we practice forgiveness with oth-ers, they will be more forgiving of us. If communities such as a business can live in forgiveness with each other, there will be less friction.

It took practice, but Amy stopped absorbing Gayle's barbs as inten-tional. Although Gayle appeared to be trying to get Amy pushed out of the company by attaching her to a failing project, Amy refused to feel like a failure. The more Gayle snarked, the more Amy cajoled. At the very least, as Crowley had predicted, the intensity of their interactions diminished.

But then a series of little miracles happened. First, the radioactive project that seemed doomed to ruin the career of anybody who touched it took on new, elevated prestige. In part, this turnaround was possible because of Amy's unsentimental acumen in quickly sorting out what about the project could be saved and what needed to be tossed. Also, as it turned out, the person who had been solely in charge of the project before Amy revealed himself to be very competent—just not well man-aged. Amy and her new project partner worked together as a team so well, in fact, the resulting success was considered one of the highlights of the company's year. Most surprisingly, the formerly doomed project was renewed for another campaign and received important industry recognition at an award ceremony (the trophy did not have Gayle's name on it).

More important, unbeknownst to Amy, for months, about a half-dozen key players at the agency had spoken privately on Amy's behalf to the owner and/or the head of HR about how unfairly Amy was being treated. Cashing in their own goodwill with the owner by speaking out directly against the self-interested longtime agency managers, these conscientious colleagues risked being fired for disloyalty or insubordination by taking up Amy's cause. Nobody coordinated these men and women to complain; they decided individually that, based on what they were seeing in company meetings, somebody had to say something. As if led by the invisible hand of God, the owner then began to ask a lot of questions about how things were actually being run.

The miracle that followed did not come overnight or without resistance, but it came nonetheless. To everybody's surprise—especially Crowley's when she was told about it later—after an unscheduled all-company meeting, Gayle left "of her own accord" for greener pastures. Less is known about the other manager who had covered for Gayle, but suddenly, quietly, she was gone, too. The exit memos were dignified, but despite the many long years at the agency, there were no big parties and no big send-off. The most people were saying about Gayle in the hallway afterward was "Thank God, it's finally over."

There also was no cinematic moment of vindication for Amy—that is, she wasn't hoisted up on a chair, and there were no chants of "Rudy! Rudy! Rudy!"—but everybody knew what she had survived. A giant exhalation was felt down the same hallways that had once been a place where new ideas went to die. Around the Nespresso machine, smiles spontaneously would break out at the civility of the new environment just before somebody would comment to Amy, "It's like a miracle they're gone and you're still here."

Indeed, it was an amazing little thing to see. The expected, normal course of human events—"the Sacred Cow never loses"—had been redirected. As if God had said, "Be . . . and it is," suddenly there was freedom from office tyranny, even if it was still a long way from a Promised Land. One can choose not to believe in miracles, but to the extent that "a miracle is what seems impossible but happens anyway," a phalanx of employees independently inspired to speak on Amy's behalf to the owner felt biblically epic.

It took a lot of divine torqueing over several years in Egypt, too, but after the Ten Plagues that ravaged Pharaoh's kingdom up to the palace itself, the man who postured himself as a god finally relented in the middle of the night and conceded to Moses' demand to "Let my people go!" Pharaoh declared, "Up, depart from among my people, you and the Israelites with you! Go, worship the Eternal as you said." The last plague—the death of all the firstborn sons of the Egyptians—had finally done him in.

Per Ibn Kathir, Pharaoh's advisors then told the king that before it was too late, he should kill Moses "with the sons of those who believe, but let their women live." Knowing of the plot, however, God warned Moses to leave with the first wave of the approximately 600,000 refugees and their livestock, and the assassination was thwarted. As Moses and Aaron led the Children of Israel out of bondage, in the Bible, Pharaoh added a request to a departing Moses in a fit of melancholy: "And may you bring a blessing upon me also!"

What was meant exactly by Pharaoh's final line to Moses is debatable. Maybe he looked around his country and saw that his stubborn hubris had done nothing more than devastate his own people. All the crops, the livestock, and the firstborn male of every non-Jewish Egyptian family were dying, or dead, including the king's own son (the death of the firstborns is not mentioned in the qur'anic narrative). Perhaps Pharaoh's realization that his resistance to the Hebrew God had killed his child came with the understanding that he was not a deity after all. Perhaps Pharaoh knew instinctively that he would be unable to repair the damage that resulted from his cruel arrogance without a true higher power.

Amy took no pleasure in knowing that Gayle's life would never be the same; Moses did not gloat over Pharaoh. In keeping with a key concept in Judaism that seeks to repair the world in the image of the divine kingdom, the impulse to celebrate at another's expense is understandable but should be resisted. Moses took the first steps toward reconciliation when he and Aaron left the palace with no further rancor or retribution. As it states in Proverbs, "When your enemy falls, do not rejoice."

The Qur'an has a similar position on how one should behave concerning a vanquished adversary. In the story of the Queen of Sheba (*Saba*), her people worshiped the sun and other objects. On receiving the invitation of King Solomon to come to him, the Queen of Sheba asks her courtiers to recommend how she should respond. While they extol the strength of their possessions and powers, the Queen offers her own assessment, saying, "Surely the kings, when they enter a town, ruin it and make the noblest of its people to be low." The invitation from Solomon seemed to be more gracious and purposeful.

When the Queen finally arrives at Solomon's palace and is impressed with not only the glamour of the palace but also the character and wisdom of Solomon, she submits to God and abandons her local gods and related rituals. In her rejection of what she believed earlier, the Queen affirmed her own assessment that good rulers, after defeating their enemies, do not ruin their towns or humiliate the noblest of the town's people.

Much later in history, when Muhammed entered Makkah (Mecca) after vanquishing people who had tormented him and his followers until they were forced to flee from their homes, the prophet forgave the city's inhabitants. The most basic lesson in the story of the Queen of Sheba and the conduct of Muhammed, then, offered in the context of a war, conquest, or retaliation, is that destruction for the sake of destruction, or humiliation for the sake of humiliation, is not permissible in the eyes of Allah. Humility in victory is just as important as humility in defeat. Elsewhere, the Qur'an admonishes believers to stop fighting once the enemy is inclined to make peace.

At the social level, an often-quoted verse of the Qur'an refers to dealing with enmity: "But [since] good and evil cannot be equal, repel [evil] with something that is better and lo! He between whom and yourself was enmity [may then become] as though he had [always] been close [unto you], a true friend!" When nation-states are inclined to war because one has wronged the other, is it not possible that the aggrieved nation-state responds with actions that are better, more beneficial to their peoples, more ethical, more strategically conceived to achieve the stated objective than a jingoistic call to arms?

In the Bible, the once-enslaved Hebrews do not leave Egypt empty-handed, but it was not a fortune collected at the tip of a spear. As Moses began the trek toward the Land of Milk and Honey, Egyptians voluntarily gave the former slaves gold and other valuables as an incentive to get them out of Egypt as fast as possible. Perhaps besides fearing more retribution from God, the Egyptians were trying to make reparations to their former captives because, as the Qur'an' states, "So, God warded off the evils that they plotted against (Moses), while a dreadful doom encompassed the followers of the Pharaoh." Either way, the Egyptians crowdsourced the Israelites with jewels, fabrics, unleavened bread, and other necessities for the journey, and the Israelites left without any physical harm to their former masters.

From the theological perspective of Judaism, Christianity, and Islam, God always challenges humanity to be better toward one's tormentors than they deserve. As it says so pithily in Proverbs, "If your enemy is hungry, give him food to eat; if he is thirsty, give him water to drink. In doing this, you will heap burning coals of shame on their heads, and the Lord will reward you." The people sought no retribution against the Egyptians.

Because humanity always has been in a state of disrepair, men and women who have been wronged can either humbly work toward making it better or risk making it worse in the name of "justice." All three traditions hold up the belief that God calls us to make it better. No prophet says that choosing reconciliation over revenge will be easy, but everybody agrees that in doing so, we will be blessed.

For example, by leading with gratitude and forgiveness, Amy attempted to defuse her tension with Gayle and make a difficult situation less acrimonious. Amy was unaware that this humility—however painful—was noticed by her co-workers, who then unpredictably came to her defense with the people who could actually bring about change.

Yet tyrants are not known to give up so easily. When Pharaoh later reconsidered the loss of his slave workforce, he decided to break his contract with Moses once more and forego his requested blessing from God. One can only wonder how the Egyptian kingdom might have recovered if Pharaoh had remained true to his word. Instead, all the king's horses and all the king's men took off for the desert to stop Moses and re-enslave the Jews before they could reach the Red Sea.

Which is why Moses' greatest test of servant leadership was yet to come. Between a regretful Pharaoh amassing his army on Moses' rear flank to kill him and the subsequent tension within his own ranks due to fear and uncertainty dead ahead, Moses needed to find new levels of skilled communication to keep his company of men, women, and children from abandoning their mission before it could even get started.

And if all of that wasn't hard enough, soon Moses would have a showdown with a giant Sacred Cow of his own. In the process, this encounter will raise one of the most difficult questions in the biblical text concerning Moses' leadership.

THE MOSAIC OF CHAPTER 4

1. In Judaism, each of us is obligated to forgive somebody who has wronged us if the offender asks with sincere contrition, but forgiveness also can be offered regardless.

2. According to Muslim tradition, the obligation on the faithful is to make seventy excuses for an offender's behavior—that is, resist assuming the worst possible motives and treat every infraction as a misunderstanding.

3. In Christianity, on the subject of forgiving, Jesus says, "I tell you, not just seven times, but seventy times seven."

4. From the theological perspective of Judaism, Christianity, and Islam, God always challenges humanity to be better toward one's tormentors than they deserve.

5. What is a true miracle? In Islam, the best answer is "A faith in a power beyond human imagination."

6. "A miracle is what seems impossible but happens anyway."

7. Jewish tradition dating back to post-biblical times makes it clear that all miracles transcend human action.

5

Moses and Communicating with the Children of Israel 2.0

Few generations have taken as much guff for their unique group characteristics (or maybe clichés) than Millennials: They want to be able to set their own schedule and work hours, they want to share their opinions on everything even if it doesn't affect them, and they are conflict-averse. Sure, Millennial workspaces look like the break rooms of Baby Boomer–oriented organizations, and true, Millennials have eschewed the traditional dozen donuts by the Mr. Coffee machine for a locally sourced kale salad dispenser next to the sustainable latte maker, but business in America is still getting done and, arguably, better than ever before. Millennials are thriving under leaders they admire, doing work they feel has a greater purpose than just personal enrichment, and communicating with a frequency and style that is new in Western modernity.

But the Millennial drive to change history, the need to front-face their leadership, to participate in their own goal-setting, and to communicate openly as a way of encouraging participation and growth, would have been very similar to the Moses-led Children of Israel. Today, transparency is one of the hallmarks of effective communication with Millennials because without it, one has no way of knowing who is telling the truth, but this model is as old as the pyramids. Unpacking the Moses narrative with attention to mass and interpersonal messaging during the

Exodus reaffirms the foundational cruciality of effective communication in predicting success.

With around 600,000 people simultaneously divesting from Pharaoh's Egypt in favor of an underfunded start-up with a lofty but vague value proposition of "finding a Promised Land of Milk and Honey someday, somewhere," one can view the Exodus as a large corporate split led by a first-time CEO. The Hebrew slaves who toiled the hardest for zero ownership in Pharaoh's Egypt were suddenly full-equity partners in this new venture with a legacy name: Israel.

This chapter, then, reveals how the challenges of transitioning a large slave population (roughly the size of Baltimore, Maryland, supposedly) to self-autonomy inform the difficulties that many present-day organizations face as they grow larger and more focused on their mission. Both literally and figuratively, there was no roadmap for Moses as he pushed himself to bring all the Israelites to the Promised Land. Mindful of when God first spoke to him through the burning bush, saying, "Since you tend people's sheep with such overwhelming love, I swear you shall be the shepherd of my sheep, Israel," Moses wanted all of God's people to prosper.

Entering the wilderness with nothing more than what they could carry or pull must have been terrifying. Captivity was brutal and cruel, but there was a certain predictability to it. Staring up at the night sky, exposed to the elements, it is easy to imagine how some Israelites might have romanticized their past and had thoughts of turning back. It would take imagination and ambition to survive the desert hardships toward a greater goal; yet entrepreneurship is not for everybody. Some people talk a good game about leaving a dead-end job and reaching for the stars, but, deep down, something about the stability of slaving away in a cubicle appeals to them.

In the rearview mirror, the country the Jews left behind had devolved since Joseph originally invited his eleven brothers, his father Israel, and all of his extended family on a giant chain-migration visa to Egypt. Then the kingdom was forward thinking, generous, and peaceful. Thanks to

Joseph's God-inspired visions, the Egyptian national storehouses were so full they had enough to share with famished foreigners. Egypt's ancient fiscal policy of sharing its surplus with those in need guaranteed God's blessing on the land.

But by the time of the events referred to in the Bible as the Exodus (which is recounted in the biblical book of Exodus), the Egypt of Moses' day had been corrupted by the vanity and paranoia of a succession of narcissistic kings who fanned the flames of bigotry and xenophobia to control the people. As much as the unnamed pharaoh whom Moses confronted demonized the Jews, he also refused to let them go. After breaking his promises to let the Hebrew slaves go free nine previous times, this Pharaoh accepted God's reluctant deliverance of the Tenth Plague, the death of every firstborn male child in his kingdom.

Starting at the stroke of midnight, the Bible says the loss was complete from the Pharaoh's oldest son to the firstborn of the lowliest prisoner in the king's dungeon—even the livestock. Like Thanos snapping his fingers in *Avengers: Infinity War*, "there was loud wailing in Egypt, for there was not a house without someone dead." Seen as a bookend to the pharaonic decree issued shortly after Moses' birth that all male Jewish babies in Egypt were to be murdered, the angel of death passed over the houses of any Hebrew household that smeared lamb's blood on its door. This time, the Israelite boys were spared.

It should be noted that although the Qur'an does not mention the Tenth Plague, the absence does not detract from the same underlying lesson in Judaism and Christianity: God is the supreme, omnipotent power. The two narratives do not differ in their essence. The Muslim perspective is focused on Pharaoh's resistance to recognizing a power greater than himself. Though only nine plagues (or "signs") appear in the Qur'an, Muslims neither confirm nor contradict the biblical narrative surrounding the Tenth Plague.

Many people of faith are uncomfortable with the Tenth Plague. The Bible makes no mention of any deaths from the first nine plagues. The plagues were no doubt awful, but they were intended as a sign to the people about worshiping a false god in Pharaoh, not a death penalty on innocent citizens. The guilty one was Pharaoh. A question of proportionality often arises in Christian apologetics: "If it was wrong for the pharaohs to enslave and brutalize thousands of innocent Jews, then how could it be right for Moses to work with God to kill thousands of innocent Egyptian boys?" The best response may be nonlinear.

One answer to this question can be found in the Exodus narrative as explicated by the rabbinical sages of the Talmud, the scholars who have contributed to thousands of years of biblical instruction. After Moses parts the Red Sea (also known as the Sea of Reeds) and after Pharaoh's troops pursue God's people only to drown, Moses' sister, the prophetess Miriam, gives thanks to God by singing the "Song of the Sea" while young maidens perform a victory dance on the shore. So much for Proverbs: "When your enemy falls, do not rejoice." God is not amused.

Essentially, God flags Moses and Miriam for an excessive touchdown celebration. God admonishes the revelers harshly, saying, "My handiwork are drowning in the sea and you are singing?" This emphasizes that God has compassion for all human beings; the Egyptians were his creation as well. God was on the side of the Jews until Miriam broke out in a taunting song and took pleasure in the deaths of so many. God is irritated at that indulgence. This incident is also an example of how the Children of Israel had a lot to learn before they could experience success as a nation. Judging by the Bible and the Qur'an, each day brought another life lesson in the desert. Often, the lessons were about themselves.

For example, when Pharaoh let the people go, God did not lead the Israelites on the shorter path from Egypt because the direct route to the Red Sea would have gone through contested territory where the refugees might have been attacked. Instead, God chose a more circuitous road, saying, "If the people face war, they might change their minds and return to Egypt." Although the Israelites left Egypt feeling ready for battle, God knew they were not militarily trained or battle tested.

The bones of their patriarch, Joseph, led the way. In a foreshadowing of the famous Ark of the Covenant, the Israelites brought the remains of

Joseph from Egypt because he had made the ancestors of the Israelites swear an oath generations earlier: "You can count on God to come to your aid if you carry my bones up with you from this place." The honor of being Joseph's bones-keeper went to Moses.

On the first night, the people camped on the edge of the desert. By day, a cloud pillar guided them on their way; after dark, a pillar of fire watched over them and gave the people the option to keep moving. No surprise, the Bible tells us, the omnipresent pillar of cloud/fire was the Lord guiding them toward the Red Sea.

Having regretted his largesse, Pharaoh would soon give chase with his entire army, including all of his chariots and all his horsemen. Going straight through the contested territory instead of around it allowed for Pharaoh's troops to close the gap on the refugees. Through Moses, God instructed the people to decamp from where they were and double back to another place on the shore of the Red Sea in order to fool Pharaoh's army into thinking that they were lost and going in circles. The Qur'an specifies that Pharaoh had sent spies ahead who reported back to the king that the Israelites would be easy prey.

With about 600,000 people amassed on the beach, the Israelites far outnumbered the pursuing Egyptians. Yet when the Israelites looked up and saw the Egyptians in the distance marching toward them, they were terrified and cried out to the Lord. Turning to Moses, they said, sarcastically, "Was it because there were no graves in Egypt that you brought us to the desert to die? What have you done to us by bringing us out of Egypt? Didn't we say to you in Egypt, 'Leave us alone; let us serve the Egyptians'? It would have been better for us to serve the Egyptians than to die in the desert!"

This problem of adjusting to a new culture of self-reliance was just what God had been worried about after the split from Pharaoh. Despite having witnessed the miraculous signs that had led to their freedom, forgetting that a giant cloud pillar was leading them in the daytime while a pillar of fire gave them comfort at night, the mere sight of the king's army was enough for the Israelites to panic. According to the qur'anic summation by Ibn Kathir, despite Moses' best attempts to calm his people, even Joshua, son of Nun, his loyal young assistant, was losing faith the closer the army came: "In front of us is this impassable barrier, the sea, and behind us, the enemy; surely death cannot be avoided!" The Qur'an says Moses stood silently and waited for God.

Or, as the Bible describes it, Moses yelled loudly, "Do not be afraid. Stand firm, and you will see the deliverance the Lord will bring you today. The Egyptians you see today you will never see again. The Lord will fight for you; you need only to be still." Or maybe both. The Qur'an says that as the people began to lose control, God inspired Moses to strike the sea with his staff, but the Bible account includes God's command to "Raise your staff and stretch out your hand over the sea to divide the water so that the Israelites can go through the sea on dry ground." Once more, God promised to expedite Pharaoh's decision process by hardening his heart so that the whole skirmish would be over faster. Moses then wielded his staff. First, the winds came, then the sea began to swirl and spin, and suddenly the waters parted to reveal a pathway dry enough for the people to walk across.

To briefly revisit the chapter on the acceptance of the miracles even for nonbelievers, agnostic polymath Charles Pellegrino argues that, given the planet-shaking volcanic eruption on the Greek island of Thera in 1600 BCE, tsunamis impacting the Red Sea would have been a natural occurrence. If true, the refugees standing on the banks would have been positioned to take advantage of the suddenly receding waters before they came rushing back. As the world witnessed during the 2004 Indian Ocean tsunamis that killed more than 200,000 people in twelve countries, the water is deadliest when it returns. Archeological evidence suggests that tsunamis from the quaking earth were roughly concurrent with the Exodus timeline.

"The tsunamis varied in height depending on the shape of the shore, but they certainly struck Egypt, as did the crop-killing dust," Pellegrino claims. "In one part of Turkey, the waves were able to carve out channeled scablands thirty miles inland." The same would have been true for the Egyptian side of the Mediterranean. "This suggests a wave that, at the shore, would have been raised to the height of the Washington Monument. Estimated wave height from Thera at the Nile Delta would have been forty to sixty feet." To the extent that the archeological record can be confirmed, the subsequent wall of water that returned after the Red Sea receded would have been so high it would have made Cecil B. DeMille's movie depiction look like it was shot in a kiddie pool.

Pellegrino adds this footnote: "Interestingly, for a while, monotheism takes root even in Egypt itself, during the eighteenth dynasty. Thera was the greatest volcanic upheaval civilization has ever seen. Something quite dramatic must have occurred, to cause such change, including apparent doubt in the old gods."

The reader likely knows the rest: The Lord held the Egyptian army back until the last refugee was safe on the other side, the king's horses and the chariots becoming stuck and the men confused, but before Pharaoh could retreat, the water flowed back and covered the entire army that had followed the Israelites into the sea. Spoiler alert: None of them survived. It was an ominous moment. Seeing no way out, Pharaoh exclaimed in the qur'anic narrative, "'I believe that there is no god worthy of worship except Allah in Whom the children of Israel believe, and I am of those who surrender to Him.' But Allah did not accept this declaration from the tyrant."

Given the number of chances that Pharaoh had to do the right thing and lead his people into prosperity instead of using his power and resources to do evil, God had no choice but to let the parted sea close back on the king and his army. All else had failed; failure is not a victory for God. God felt the fear and agony of so much life drowning under the weight of their own armor just as much as God felt the joy and relief of the Children of Israel who were now finally, completely free. That's when Miriam and her back-up singers got up on a rock overlooking the carnage, and God cringed.

It is in this post-Exodus period in the desert, on the other side of the Red Sea, that Moses' real culture-changing work as a servant leader began. For this separate enterprise to be successful, a new corporate identity had to be established. Who were they, these Children of Israel? Could they shed the scarred skin of their former enslavement? What were their defining characteristics as God worshipers that contrasted them with other groups? What would their corporate values be as they formed a new autonomous body? What could they be expected to withstand? How could the Israelites come out of this deadly showdown with Pharaoh's army with actions that were more beneficial, more ethical, and more strategically conceived to be better aligned with their core beliefs?

In short, the transformation of generations of oppressed, beaten individuals who had subsisted more than they had existed into a new creation that could stand on its own, defend itself, and thrive into perpetuity would require a most humble man to both serve and lead 600,000 people not just out of slavery but also out of brokenness. Moses, a solitary shepherd who lacked confidence in public speaking, would have to embrace the challenge of effective communication on an unimaginable scale.

The Qur'an lays out the hallmarks of effective communication this way: kindness, truthfulness, and verification. Being kind and gentle in all manner of interpersonal interaction is the underlying directive in the Divine Message. God reminds the Children of Israel of the solemn pledge He had accepted from them, reminding them that among other acts of obedience, "You shall speak unto all people in a kindly way." While encouraging the giving of charity, God also reminds the believers that a "kind word and the veiling of another's want is better than a charitable deed followed by hurt." Similarly, God encourages the giving of charity and sharing of sustenance, but if one cannot give because one is oneself in need, believers are advised to "at least speak unto them with gentle speech."

This was true even when God commanded Moses to go to Pharaoh in the first place. Although God armed Moses with authority and miraculous powers to impress the Pharaoh, God also counseled Moses to speak to Pharaoh with "gentle speech that perhaps he may be reminded or fear [God]."

The flip side of being truthful in communication is to verify what is being communicated as being or not being the truth. This is more so if the communication one receives comes from a source that may not be of good character, or the communication itself may be slanderous or suspicious. In such cases, God advises the receiver of such communication to "use your discernment, lest you hurt people unwittingly and afterward be filled with remorse for what you have done." Even when communication is not slanderous and simply a record of what has happened, one must seek verification from a different, unbiased source.

In Judaism, the approach to communication is very much the same: "The words of the wise are spoken gently." Another great dictum of Jewish tradition is "Do not hate your brother in your heart; talk to him and let him know what's on your mind." Working out problems is not a one-shot event, either. God calls us to consider whether the person we owe an apology to is not receptive at first because they have something else going on. "If someone does not forgive you, keep asking for forgiveness," the saying goes, because each of us may hold a grudge longer than others.

With regard to best communication practices, the Christian-specific scriptures either echo or rephrase the dominant Hebrew wisdom literature from the Old Testament section of the Christian Bible with a few interesting additions, such as in the book of James. Here, the man identified as the little brother of Jesus extends the concept of transparent communication to include our actions as well as our language: "Be *doers* of the word, and not merely hearers who deceive themselves." It would be nice if everybody who talked the talk also walked the walk.

If that seems unremarkable, consider that past military-style models of business leadership in the United States stressed communications between those at the top and the rank and file at the bottom were to be mostly on a "need-to-know" basis. If the old military model was about "truth management," where one was only privy to the inner workings of a company after moving up the ladder, then the new modes of "truth telling" are intended to build employee loyalty and trust from the lowest rung.

In fact, the necessity and former popularity of employee unions were predicated on legendary adversarial relationships between informed management and labor that was kept in the dark. For a century, labor could only get a seat at the tables of power through collective bargaining. One reason why unions have lost traction with the American workforce over the years might be linked to an increase in employee satisfaction regarding how operations are being run. Improved, authentic, two-way communication between the factory floor and the front office has thawed management/employee relations.

With the dependence on constant telephonic and computer communications such as cell phones, email, and video-conferencing systems over the last twenty years, however, face-to-face communication within organizations has become something that some companies have to maintain with great intention. One media company in Minnesota went so far as to establish a new norm: If it takes more than two emails to resolve an issue with a colleague, close your laptop, get out of your chair, and go work it out with him or her in person.

Although Millennials have taken corporate transparency, two-way communication, and horizontal management/employee relationships to new heights, their well-known generational reliance on technology can sometimes lead to them taking physical face-to-face opportunities for granted. To combat this tendency, typical Millennial-focused offices are designed to optimize group interaction through the arrangement of workspaces, office flow, and luxurious break/play areas.

This arrangement is important because the lack of physical face-to-face communication between peers and superiors can often hamper a career. In the brevity of texts and the often indiscernible tone of email, the intended meaning and nuance of communication can be lost, sometimes with tragic consequences. In-person audio and facial cues can communicate more information faster and more accurately, which can be essential when discussing sensitive social and political issues without misunderstandings. Because messaging is so frequently scrutinized for both text and subtext, getting the wrong idea from impersonal electronic interactions can be a hard bell to un-ring, even if the writer assumed the recipient knew he or she was joking or intended a comment in a friendlier way than it came across.

Of course, email was not an issue in Moses' day, but that just made effective communication with 600,000 refugees an even greater challenge. Moses did benefit from one preexisting corporate structure of elders: The descendants of the twelve sons of Israel were already divided up into their twelve tribes, with the elders forming a kind of tribal council at the top. The Qur'an confirms that the refugees were affiliated according to their tribes and that the elders brought their grumbles to Moses. And there was a lot of grumbling.

For example, after the victory at the Red Sea, the 600,000 had been moving for three days straight before they arrived at a desert place called Marah, and they were thirsty. Unfortunately, the water was bitter and undrinkable. Perhaps indicative of the amount of time the Children of Israel had been in captivity, those who grumbled to Moses do not come off as very self-sufficient. Moses, like a good custodial leader, mediated the request to God nonetheless. After Moses cried out to the Lord, God drew his attention to a piece of wood on the ground. Moses took the stick and threw it into the bitter water, and it instantly became potable.

However, in the same manner that Moses was passing messages up to God from the people, God, too, was communicating incentives and rules down the chain to this nascent nation through Moses. "If you listen carefully to the Lord your God and do what is right in God's eyes," the prophet relayed, "if you pay attention to his commands and keep all his decrees, 'I will not bring on you any of the diseases I brought on the Egyptians, for I am the Lord, who heals you.'"

A few days later, Moses was guided to a resting place with twelve springs, one for each tribe, and seventy palm trees to provide some shade. The Qur'an credits Moses with creating the twelve springs by striking a rock with his staff, something Moses also would do later in the Bible timeline (the importance of that second version will become evident further in the narrative), so the theme is the same: Moses is staying just one step ahead of his constantly needy people. This is the burden that Rabbis Yehoshua and Gamaliel pinpointed in the remark "Woe to the generation whose *provider* you are, and woe to the ship whose *captain* you are." At this stage, Moses was leading the people by serving them even though the neediness of the former slaves was exhausting.

Unfortunately, Moses' best efforts to unify the flock did not prevent the sheep from going everywhere. The Qur'an puts it bluntly: "In spite of Pharaoh's death, he left a bad influence on the souls of the children of Israel," it says. "It was difficult for the years of oppression and intense humility to pass easily. He had made them accustomed to humbling themselves and submitting to someone other than Allah. He had so suppressed their souls and spoiled their nature that they began to torture Moses out of ignorance and obstinacy."

The grumbling grew louder and even more directed at Moses and Aaron when, on the fifteenth day of the second month out of captivity, the food supplies that the people had brought with them were running out. "The Israelites said to them, 'If only we had died by the Lord's hand in Egypt! There we sat around pots of meat and ate all the food we wanted, but you have brought us out into this desert to starve this entire assembly to death.'" Somehow, the very humble and reluctant servant leader who brought them out of bondage was becoming a threat in the minds of some vocal Israelites.

In a fairly sophisticated description of the theoretical psychological phenomenon known as "transference," the Qur'an argues that, in fact, the Children of Israel were suffering from a kind of Stockholm syndrome related to their captivity. Even though "the miracle of the parting of the sea was still fresh in their minds, [and] damp sea sands were still stuck on their soles," as the Qur'an puts it, the people were subconsciously identifying with their captors to the extent that when they passed by some desert dwellers who were worshiping idols, they were jealous. Although it was Allah who deserved their recognition as the one, true God, "they looked to Moses for him to specify a god for them to worship as those other people did. . . . They missed the ancient idolatry which they had lived with during the reign of Pharaoh."

This means that despite all of the care and feeding, the Israelites had not bonded to God directly but only to Moses, who had been sent by God to be their custodial leader and intermediary. After years of believing that their prayers for release had been ignored, the Children of Israel gave up on traditional Jewish theology, which taught that all believers had direct access to God.

In effect, despite their protests that they wanted Moses to designate an idol to which they could bow down, the people already had idolized Moses in the purest sense of the verb. Moses was something the people could see and touch, not unlike some cow made out of gold that they might have seen in Egypt. God was an abstract concept or, at best, a cloud or a fire, but they could take their grievances to Moses and yell at him. The Children of Israel triangulated their two-way communication to Moses, taking a hard pass on their right to confront God. The Qur'an does not record Moses' response to that clear communication from the people, if he had any.

Per both holy books, though, God was listening every time the people came to Moses, so the Lord said, "I will rain down bread from heaven for you. The people are to go out each day and gather enough for that day. In this way, I will test them and see whether they will follow my instructions." This sets the table for the famous Bible story of "manna," an unknown white, flaky substance that tasted like wafers made with honey that started to appear on the desert ground with the morning dew. Each Israelite was to gather their fill except on the Sabbath (on average, about six pounds daily). Manna could be baked, boiled, or eaten raw, but it could not be hoarded because it would spoil. Manna was plentiful and nutritious, and it sustained them for the next forty years, along with the occasional pigeon or other meat.

One might think that God giving them, this day, their daily bread would have been a breakthrough in the Israelites-God relationship.

Instead, they turned back on Moses and complained the very moment they perceived lack. When the people were thirsty again, for example, they argued with Moses and said, "Give us water to drink." When Moses replied, "Why do you quarrel with me? Why do you put the Lord to the test?" the people got personal again, essentially blaming Moses for freeing them: "'Why did you bring us up out of Egypt to make us and our children and livestock die of thirst?' No matter what Moses did, the Israelites quarreled more and tested the Lord, saying, 'Is the Lord with us or against us?'"

But where the Bible portrays the Israelites negatively in subtext, the Qur'an is much more explicit on how slavery had corrupted their minds, stunted their spiritual growth, and made them petulant. The Qur'an lists how Allah delivered the people from captivity, drowned their cruel overlord, and also kept the skies cloudy overhead to protect them from the scorching heat. Yet, for all of God's generosity, certain mean-spirited rebels within the group were instigating trouble. To them, even free, abundant, easily collected manna wasn't enough. They wanted more menu options.

The Qur'an identifies that some disruptive Israelites were "disgusted with this food; they desired onions, garlic, beans, and lentils, which were traditional Egyptian foods. That is why the children of Israel asked Prophet Moses to pray to Allah to make the earth produce these foods," but because Moses was wise, he could tell what the real issue was. Moses knew that although Pharaoh was dead, he still had a grip on the souls of many of the older Israelites, and so the prophet "admonished them for oppressing themselves and for their desire to return to a life of humiliation in Egypt."

As the leader for the Exodus, Moses must have struggled with a creeping realization early on. No matter how hard he tried to get all 600,000 Israelites to buy in to this new corporate culture where each person could establish their own relationship with God and be responsible for their own salvation, the evidence was mounting that some would never rise to the task. Dissent in the desert would be one thing, but nation-building success would only be possible through unity. What purpose would it serve to go through all this pain to establish this new enterprise, to be granted this amazing Promised Land, and then have it fall into disarray, fall to enemy hands, or, worse, fall to civil war?

Once again, the Qur'an is less euphemistic than the Bible. Per Muhammed, there was only just so much whining Allah could stand before a judgment was reached: Those Israelites whose nature had been "corrupted by the Egyptians" needed to be culled from the group. As a result, Allah decreed, the Children of Israel must wander in the wilderness "until this generation had died or become senile and had created another generation, a generation which had not been defeated from within and which could fight and score victory."

"A generation defeated from within" is the perfect way to describe what others might call a cancer on an organization. Anybody who has worked with somebody in a group who puts down the company, the boss, and his or her job or talks incessantly about how much better the organization used to be understands the toxicity of that environment. After a merger or a takeover, some people will get swept forward by the momentum who would have been better left behind. Humble leaders such as Moses may even be too forgiving with employees who have an old boss or an old system with a grip on their soul. New entities run the risk of being defeated from within if the first generation of workers is defeated from within themselves. It would be unfair to say that Moses was conflict-averse—he had an unbeaten record in his showdowns with Pharaoh—but so far, Moses' patience was not paying off.

Accepting failure is the hardest part of leadership, but failing to adjust to new realities only compounds that challenge. Delaying the Exodus until a new gestalt among the Jews could be formed was a necessary evil; no organization can move forward if its people are looking back. Following God's plan that the 600,000 cannot enter the Promised Land until a new generation had been forged that was up to the challenge of nation-building meant that an entire generation of Israelites would wander through the desert until enough of the older ones died or went senile. Still, a delayed launch is better than a failed one.

As the servant leader, Moses was charged with following God's call, so he would have to do his best to maintain the health and happiness of the Children of Israel for forty years, the amount of time it took between leaving Egypt and crossing over into the land that had been occupied by the Canaanites, Hittites, Amorites, Perizzites, Hivites, and Jebusites.

Whether it truly was forty years of wandering in the desert is difficult to say because, in biblical numerology, forty is used symbolically to describe any great period of trial or tribulation (the Qur'an has it slightly differently). It's not a coincidence that in the story of Noah, it rained for forty days and forty nights, or that before receiving the Ten Commandments, Moses fasted for forty days and forty nights, or that this was the length of the temptation of Christ preceding the start of his ministry. When the reader sees forty, the implication should just be "a really long, difficult time." Even with the elders of the Twelve Tribes of Israel working with him, Moses would need more than divine authority to keep the peace between the people while a generation learned to front-face God, to become invested in the success of the mission (not just personal enrichment), and to communicate openly as a way of encouraging increased group participation and growth and avoiding conflict and creating community.

Fortuitously, the Bible says that around this time, Moses got an unexpected consultation from a visitor from the home office. Now that things in the desert were settling down and Moses knew he would be moving the Children of Israel around the desert for a generation, he had sent for his wife, Zipporah, to join him with their two sons, Gershom and Eliezer. What apparently surprised Moses was that Jethro, the priest of Midian and his father-in-law, sent word ahead that he would be coming with his daughter and grandsons on the journey because he had heard so much about what Moses had done for his people.

The reunion was well needed, it seems, and Moses was so grateful to see Jethro that he bowed down and kissed him upon arrival. While relaxing in the shade of a tent, "Moses told his father-in-law about everything the Lord had done to Pharaoh and the Egyptians for Israel's sake and about all the hardships they had met along the way and how the Lord had saved them." Not only did Jethro enjoy hearing the exciting stories of escape, near capture, and their rescue at the Red Sea, but he also seemed to renounce his previous association with the god of the Midianites when he said, "Praise be to the Lord, who rescued you from the hand of the Egyptians and of Pharaoh, and who rescued the people from the hand of the Egyptians. Now I know that the Lord is greater than all other gods, for he did this to those who had treated Israel arrogantly."

Then, the Bible says, Jethro brought a "burnt offering and other sacrifices to God." According to tradition, these are two different things. To commemorate the Lord's prowess, Moses' success, and their reunion, Jethro set aside one animal for God to be consumed by fire completely on a makeshift altar—that's the "burnt offering." The other "sacrifices" would have been other animals to be barbecued and shared communally after the burnt offering was reduced to ashes. Basically, it was a big party, and God got to eat first. Aaron was invited, of course, and with him came all the elders of all the tribes of Israel to celebrate a meal with Jethro in the presence of God.

The next morning, though, it was back to work. With Jethro observing, Moses took his seat as the servant leader to all the clans to serve as the judge for the people, settling disputes and making rulings based on God's word from morning into the night. At the end of it all, Jethro was dismayed. "When his father-in-law saw all that Moses was doing for the people," the Bible states, Jethro asked, "What is this you are doing for the people? Why do you alone sit as judge, while all these people stand around you from morning till evening?"

Moses' humble answer is sincere, but today we also might recognize in Moses a tendency to be either a "fixer" personality type—that is, somebody who has a strong need to help or rescue others because it confirms their self-worth—or even a bit of a control freak. Moses answered Jethro, "Because the people come to me to seek God's will.

Whenever they have a dispute, it is brought to me, and I decide between the parties and inform them of God's decrees and instructions." Because of his humility, Moses might have gotten stuck in a myopic cycle in which he was burning himself out being overly dutiful, but somewhere along the line, Moses also might have come to believe he was the only one who could handle a disputatious people. The tendency to think of oneself as the only one who can do a job right should be as suspect today as it was then because micromanaging fosters codependency and/ or infantilizes the very people you're trying to help. In Moses' case, how would a generation of Israelites break out of the mental captivity that had gripped them if Moses alone was doing all the heavy lifting of running the society?

Jethro's gentle but firm response is so perfect that it is timeless; Jethro might as well have been recording a self-help video for his YouTube channel. Word for word, according to the Bible, Jethro said, "What you are doing is not good. You and these people who come to you will only wear yourselves out. The work is too heavy for you; you cannot handle it alone." As humble and wise as Moses was, Jethro was telling him that trying to be the primary administrator was his blind spot. We all have blind spots. Sometimes it takes bluntness to nudge us back in the right direction. Even if the truth hurts sometimes, there is no sin in candor.

In any organization, being blunt in communication is useful as long as one intends to be straightforward and to the point without being unnecessarily offensive or forceful. One of the key teachings of Judaism is to turn an adversary into a friend. However, being blunt can be unproductive if one uses truth in a degrading manner that merely pulls the other person down. In discourse designed to persuade others or to convince them in an argument, the recommended manner of communication is to engage the other "with wisdom and goodly exhortation, and argue with them in the most kindly manner." The goal of all communication must be to offer and receive correct, relevant, and constructive information. Jethro had a plan.

"Listen now to me and I will give you some advice, and may God be with you," Jethro prefaced:

> You must be the people's representative before God and bring their disputes to God. Teach them his decrees and instructions, and show them the way they are to live and how they are to behave. But select capable men from all the people—men who fear God, trustworthy men who hate dishonest gain—and appoint them as officials over thousands, hundreds, fifties and tens. Have them serve as judges for the people at all times, but have them bring every difficult case to you; the simple cases they can decide themselves. That will make your load lighter, because they will share it with you. If you do this, and God so commands, you will be able to stand the strain, and all these people will go home satisfied.

For the second time in Moses' life, Jethro had set him on the right path of the shepherd. After Moses freed the Hebrew tribes from their enslavement and led them to safety when their backs were against the Red Sea, Moses might have gotten a little lost himself dealing with conflict along the way. Moses took in all of Jethro's feedback. Although in some ways it meant a diminished role for him, Moses had enough emotional intelligence to recognize that without this new structure, the movement toward a new nation could all fall apart just as easily by resisting more delegation as it would by rushing an unprepared populace to the Promised Land.

Listening and responding to criticism is often the most difficult aspect of personal communication because few people know how to offer criticism correctly. Instead of confining their assessments and suggestions to insightful ways for the other person to build on their own strengths, many critics cannot resist crossing personal lines and inserting less-than-constructive commentary intended to change, but not necessarily improve, the receiver. Usually, feedback—the art of observing some potential areas of improvement without ruining the other person's self-esteem—is all that is needed to be helpful.

Because so many critics mistakenly believe that it's OK to crush somebody with harsh, destructive comments as long as it will be beneficial to them in the long run, they do not understand why their criticism is not received well. For the listener to be receptive to the criticism, the critic must be empathetic, engaged, and patient. One has to be empathetic in order to place value on how the criticism will be accepted. One has to be engaged in order to share opinions and points of view in a sincere manner. One has to be patient so that the recipient will have time to absorb the observations in the right context. Since invective is too often passed off as constructive criticism, most people are resistant to criticism. Jethro, however, made no insinuations about Moses' character or personality; he just fed back to the prophet a fair assessment of what he surmised based on his daylong observations of the administration of the Israelites and his respect for Moses' abilities.

Like any enduring organization, the nation of Israel was forming in stages, and the next phase required the co-creator to be a better delegator. Per Jethro, the next steps were to choose capable men from all Israel and make them "leaders of the people, officials over thousands, hundreds, fifties and tens. They served as judges for the people at all times. The difficult cases they brought to Moses, but the simple ones they decided themselves." This encouraged more growth through self-sufficiency, something Moses knew had been needed all along. With his work finished, Jethro returned to his own country.

To last the distance to the Land of Milk and Honey, Children of Israel 2.0 would have to run efficiently on all 600,000 cylinders, and this would require many laps around the Sinai test track. The Exodus, the Red Sea, and the falling of manna from heaven were all pivotal events, but the contribution of the outsider, Jethro, the Midianite priest, is often overlooked as the turning point toward success in the Promised Land.

By decentralizing the governing authority to the grassroots level through delegation, Moses had mollified the grumblers, the malcontents, and the troublemakers in one corporate restructuring. In working with Jethro's advice, Moses proved once more that a true leader cares more for the success of the group than his or her own status and recognition. The Israelites had survived their beta test, but they needed to maintain their forward movement if they were going to get over the mountain that stood between Israel and, well, Israel. Accomplishing all this would require Moses to ace the greatest test that every leader must face.

THE MOSAIC OF CHAPTER 5

1. God has compassion for all human beings; the Egyptians were God's creation also.
2. Manna was an unknown white, flaky substance that tasted like wafers made with honey that started to appear on the desert ground with the morning dew. Manna could be baked, boiled, or eaten raw, but it could not be hoarded because it would spoil.
3. Accepting failure is the hardest part of leadership, but failing to adjust to new realities only compounds that challenge.
4. Forty years wandering in the desert may be a typical, biblical use of the figurative number forty, meaning "a really long, difficult time."
5. The Children of Israel successfully grew as an organization but still needed a generation of wandering before they were ready for the Promised Land.
6. Most people do not know how to offer criticism well, but Jethro's handling of Moses regarding taking on too much is textbook feedback.
7. Growing in his ability to communicate effectively allowed Moses to grow as a leader.

6

Moses and Leadership Lessons Learned in Times of Tyrants

The nature of vital organizations is to expand. "Thank you for coming tonight. In the weeks ahead, I look forward to making our new group even smaller and less significant than it is right now," said the leader of no organization, ever. Civic groups/charities push growth to include more people and/or provide more services. Businesses of all sizes seek to increase profits steadily to build more equity and hire more workers. Religious movements recruit more members to be more socially impactful. Expansion is movement; so is succession. Organizations that do not prioritize expansion tend to enter into a form of stasis or atrophy and disappear from history.

At all the high points of the 4,000-year-span of Jewish history, there is movement. Frequently, the movement is involuntary as a result of forced dislocation, which led to suffering and then relocation and/or redemption. It starts with the patriarchs: Abraham, Isaac, and Jacob (later Israel). It continues with Israel's twelve sons who go down to Egypt, and whose descendants are enslaved for generations. It culminates with the story of Moses—namely, the liberation from Egypt, the giving of the Law at Mount Sinai, and the return to the Promised Land.

Movement in Jewish history does not stop at the end of the biblical period. In the two millennia since the last Hebrew scriptures were written, Jews constantly experienced dislocation, suffering, and relocation and/or redemption while never losing their faith or abandoning their heritage. At the hands of pharaohs of different times and places, Jews were persecuted and exiled. Two prime examples of this cycle are the expulsion of the Jews from Spain and Portugal around the time of the discovery of America and the Holocaust in Europe in the middle of the twentieth century.

The Spanish Inquisition of the Jews by the Catholic Church in 1492 began after the Moorish Kingdom of Granada fell to the Catholic monarchs Queen Isabella I of Castile and King Ferdinand II of Aragon. Up to that point, a succession of Moorish kings had granted Jews and Christians the protected status of *dhimmi* in sharia law, which meant they could live and govern their own communities. As a result, Jews, Christians, and Muslims coexisted peacefully for most of the seven centuries of Moorish rule. During this time, writing in Arabic, Maimonides (Judaism's greatest philosopher) was influenced by brilliant Muslim thinkers like Al-Farabi, Avicenna, and Averroes, as well as Aristotle. In Christian intellectual circles, Maimonides is best remembered as having a profound influence on Catholic theologian Saint Thomas Aquinas.

Those two cataclysmic events alone could have put an end to the Jewish people, but the opposite happened. The Spanish Expulsion resulted in the rebirth of Jewish life in Eastern Europe and, eventually, in the New World. The massive extermination of the Jews throughout Europe during World War II set the stage for the rebirth of Israel. Some say such events cannot be explained in purely human terms. One must go back to God's promise to Abraham of giving rise to a great and enduring nation and to the premise that the Jews have been playing a critical role in the story of human civilization.

Since its earliest days in the first century CE as a minor Jewish cult built around a humble, prophetic Galilean rabbi who performed miracles, demanded social justice, and challenged the existing table order of both the dominant Jewish temple culture and the occupying Roman authority, Christianity has been on the move, too. Many factors contributed to its rapid expansion. Again, the earliest adaptors of Christianity—such as the original twelve disciples (students) who had been called by Jesus, dubbed the anointed one, to be witnesses to his many

It is difficult to overemphasize the intellectual impact that twelfth-century Spanish polymathic rabbi/theologian/philosopher/astronomer Maimonides had on Judaism and Christianity and—to a lesser degree—on Muslim culture due to his extensive writing on medicine and astronomy. Although Maimonides was exiled from Spain during a violent, anti-Jewish swing brought on by the arrival of a radical Islamic movement that lasted for about seventy-five years, during his banishment, Maimonides' work was still studied at Islamic universities. Famously, Maimonides summarized Jewish faith in his thirteen principles. The seventh reads:

> I believe with complete faith that the prophecy of Moses, our teacher, may peace rest upon him, was true, and that he was the father of all prophets that preceded him as well as all that came after him.

By referring to prophets who preceded and succeeded Moses, Maimonides, a rational universalist who was ahead of his time, insisted that they were actual prophets and broke with what the Hebrew Bible refers to as "false prophets."

miracles—were referred to collectively as "apostles." Apostle, a word of Greek origin, means one who is "sent" or "delegated." As the word spread about Jesus, the multitude of apostles grew as well. After Jesus' crucifixion, the apostles had a sense of urgency about the return of the long-awaited Messiah, a savior for God's people against oppression and death, and they were energized to spread the message.

Becoming apostles, then, could be understood as a kind of divine respiration; first, they were drawn in, and then they were expelled out with great enthusiasm: called and then sent. The literary practices of the apostles, partially inherited from Christianity's rabbinic roots, also contributed to the sect's unprecedented growth. Apostles were media-savvy for their day. Christian converts, even in the remotest of towns, fortified each other with copies of writings passed around from other Christian communities. Disparate voices within the movement offered encouragement, in addition to discussing and debating their theological differences in formal, essay-like letters known as "epistles," which were intended to be shared aloud.

Movement punctuated by progress, relief from persecution, and promises of new beginnings also parallels the qur'anic narrative of the Muslim condition. In a time of polytheism, tribal gods, and idol worship, Muhammed's belief in the same God of Jews and Christians began to penetrate through the Meccan society, and he gained followers, especially among the weak and disadvantaged in the social order. The powerful and the prominent would not yield to reason or revelation; yet Muhammed's followers felt a sense of progress, despite opposition and hardship, a faith in the hope that ultimately truth would prevail.

Like Moses and Jesus, in many respects, Muhammed was an unlikely choice to be called to prophethood. Born into the well-respected Quraysh tribe in the Arab Peninsula, Muhammed rebelled against the cultural understanding that some people deserved privilege while others deserved to suffer. At an early age, Muhammed imagined an egalitarian society in which the rich and powerful would share the same rank and privileges as the poor and powerless. As a result, while he was one of the Quraysh, he felt apart from them in his understanding of the prevailing social norms. He respected all irrespective of their station in life and valued his relationship with them to the extent that they trusted him with their property and belongings if the need arose.

At the age of forty, having been a well-known figure among the Quraysh, life took a turn for Muhammed when he received his first revelation, a command and a charge from God to call the people of Mecca toward worship of and obedience to a single omnipotent and omnipresent Being. Muhammed was commanded to oppose the status quo; that message and all its implications ran counter to Quraysh society.

However, as Muhammed's followers grew in number and determination, the opposition likewise strengthened in its rejection of those who abandoned the local customs until Muhammed himself migrated to the city of Yathrib (now Medina). Called the *Hijra*, this movement marks the beginning of the Islamic calendar.

The migration of Muslims to Medina for safety and freedom parallels the Exodus of the Israelites from the clutches of Pharaoh. However, unlike the Israelites, who, despite entreaties by Moses, were compelled to wander in the wilderness for a generation, the *muhajireen* submitted completely to God and benefited from the leadership of Muhammed, who crafted alliances between Jewish and Muslim tribes. When the time came for the Medinian Muslims to return to their "promised land," their original home, Muslims overcame Mecca's defenses, and Muhammed entered the city as a victor. Instead of revenge, Muhammed sought reconciliation, declared amnesty, and achieved peace.

This victory is seen as proof that God chose Muhammed, as God chose Moses, at a more mature time in his life when he had achieved a level of moral purity and equanimity. Muhammed, it is said, was protected by God from any circumstance that would tarnish his character, to the extent that even before his prophethood, Muhammed was known among his detractors as *al-Amin*, or "the trustworthy." When enemies see each other as trustworthy, organic peace usually can be negotiated.

Before Muhammed, the Qur'an confirms Jesus also was sent as a messenger to resist the status quo and further the belief in the one God of Abraham during a time of Roman polytheism, local gods, and idol worship. In the Bible, the story of Jesus Christ, the disciples, and other assorted apostles is told in another narrative form called "gospels." Biblical scholars assert that while the book of Mark is rooted in the writer's Jewish heritage, the later gospels of Matthew, Luke, and John reflect a rhetorical shift toward proselytizing among non-Jewish Roman citizens who became Christianity's most fertile field for conversion. The increased, distinct use of Greek and Roman philosophical concepts and images are just a few of the editorial decisions made by the authors of what are today called New Testament texts. Although there are dissimilarities between the gospels of Christian scripture, one constant is Moses.

Christian scholars debate the degree to which these biographical contact points between the life of Jesus and the life of Moses are historical, contrived, symbolic, or incidental, but the repetition concludes they are beyond coincidental. For example, when Moses was born, Pharaoh ordered a mass killing of every Hebrew baby boy; when Jesus was born, King Herod of Judea ordered a mass killing of every Hebrew baby boy. After Moses is born, he is placed in a basket of reeds; after Jesus is born, he spends his first night in the straw of a manger. Moses is plucked from the Nile by royalty; following the Star of Bethlehem, royalty comes to visit Jesus. In order to avoid King Herod's death sentence, Jesus' family escaped to Egypt until it was safe to go home; thus, both Moses and Jesus began the most famous period of their lives after leaving the land of pharaohs: Moses parted the Red Sea; Jesus walked on water.

But as a new model for servant leadership, perhaps the Jesus-Moses connection shines brightest through a comparison of the Sermon on the Mount and the Ten Commandments. As the longest speech in the Christian part of the Bible, the Sermon on the Mount accepts the authority of Ten Commandments and yet offers Jesus' dissenting rabbinical interpretations of the Law as the basis of moral instruction for his followers. The resulting tension between honoring the biblical text and reinterpreting it is captured in Jesus' famous quote: "Do not think that I have come to abolish the Law or the Prophets. I have not come to abolish them, but to fulfill them." It is after the Sermon on the Mount that Jesus' movement is galvanized, as the Bible reports that when Jesus and the disciples came down from the mount, he was surrounded by multitudes.

Although more subtle, this image also evokes Moses at Mount Sinai, the central event in the story of Moses. Three months to the day since the Exodus began, the Israelites were camped at the foot of Mount Sinai, a smallish mountain that was hardly awe inspiring. According to Jewish tradition, God chose Mount Sinai to symbolize how humility is a prerequisite for studying the word of God. Moses went up the mountain with Aaron at the invitation of God, but not the Israelite elders. At the base of Mount Sinai, all the people could see were storm clouds, lightning, and smoke, and they heard thunder as God dictated pages of laws governing their behavior, starting with the Ten Commandments.

If God's choice of Mount Sinai as an unremarkable location to receive the Word of God was intended to emphasize humility, why choose a mountain at all? Wouldn't the metaphor have been more keenly understood if the Ten Commandments were given on a flat plain or, even better, in a valley? Such is a proposal by Hassidic Jews.

This puzzle is explained, by some, like this: While humility is important, there are also many occasions in Jewish life when a more determined and forceful approach is demanded. Personal self-sacrifice, steadfastness in the face of ridicule or contempt, and the readiness to suffer for Judaism (as Jews in Communist Russia did for many years) are responses that are sometimes required. When hearing an instruction from the Torah, we need the ability to listen. This is a rare quality because usually our own ego gets in the way. We hear our own ideas, not what is the Word of God in the Bible.

Humility is the step beyond our ego, a mood of selflessness, which makes us receptive to the Torah. Thus Jews say at the end of the daily Amidah prayer, "May my soul be to all as the dust—open my heart to your Torah." It is interesting to note that right at the beginning of the Code of Jewish Law comes the statement, "Do not be embarrassed by mockery and ridicule." As the rabbis would say, if one were to waver in observance of a Jewish law simply because of the derisive criticism of others, there would soon not be much observance of Judaism left at all. So, one needs both qualities: humility and strength. They need the ability to listen and also the firmness to be able to stand up against the current. Both qualities are expressed in the image of Mount Sinai.

Once more, the Qur'an and the Bible differ not so much in substance but in timeline regarding the Ten Commandments. According to the Qur'an, God instructed Moses to fast for thirty days *before* entering into the presence of the Lord, so he left Aaron in charge to handle any disputes, and then he ascended the mountain. After thirty days, the Qur'an says, Moses was self-conscious about his bad breath, so he ate an herbaceous plant on the ground, but this act offended God, who said to Moses, "Why did you break your fast?" Moses said, "Oh, my Lord, I disliked to speak to you with my mouth not having a pleasant smell." To which Allah replied, "Do you not know, Moses, the odor of the faster's mouth is more fragrant to me than the rose? Go back and fast ten days, then come back to me."

So, Moses fasted ten more cleansing days before receiving the Law and descended the mountain. In the Bible, Moses had been up and down the mountain a couple of times, but just before his last session, God insisted Moses should fast for forty days and forty nights. Leaving Aaron behind to settle disputes, Moses took his assistant, Joshua, son of Nun, and got his final instruction from God on a variety of important subjects. The Qur'an has this beautiful passage in which Moses kindly deputizes Aaron by saying, "Replace me among my people, act in the Right Way, and follow not the way of the *mufsideen* (mischief makers)." Both accounts end the same way: Moses had been obedient and dutiful in all his transcriptions, and "When the Lord finished speaking to Moses on Mount Sinai, he gave him the two tablets of the covenant law, the tablets of stone inscribed by the finger of God."

The last meeting between Moses and God does not end well in the Bible, however. Just before Moses would have descended triumphantly with the stone tablets, the Lord said to Moses, "Go down, because your people, whom you brought up out of Egypt, have become corrupt. They have been quick to turn away from what I commanded them and have made themselves an idol cast in the shape of a calf. They have bowed down to it and sacrificed to it and have said, 'These are your gods, Israel, who brought you up out of Egypt.'"

Indeed, according to the Bible, back at the campsite, what had transpired was almost comical, for "When the people saw that Moses was so long in coming down from the mountain, they gathered around Aaron and said, 'Come, make us gods who will go before us. As for this fellow Moses who brought us up out of Egypt, we don't know what has happened to him.'"

Putting aside the Children of Israel's comment that Moses was just some "fellow who brought us up out of Egypt," the most surprising aspect about the biblical story is that not only did Aaron comply with the rebel crowd, but he also ended up leading the mutiny by saying, "Take off the gold earrings that your wives, your sons and your daughters are wearing, and bring them to me." So all the people took off their earrings and brought them to Aaron. He took what they handed him and made it into an idol cast in the shape of a calf, fashioning it with a tool. Then they said, "These are your gods, Israel, who brought you up out of Egypt."

Even worse, it was Aaron himself who built an altar in front of the calf and announced it was time to party. "So the next day, the people rose early and sacrificed burnt offerings and presented fellowship offerings. Afterward, they sat down to eat and drink and got up to indulge in revelry."

Of course, this is not the version that Aaron told Moses when the furious lawgiver returned. In fact, in the Bible, in his defense, Aaron sounded drunk or like a character from a TV sitcom when he claimed, "You know how prone these people are to evil. They said to me, 'Make us gods who will go before us. As for this fellow Moses who brought us up out of Egypt, we don't know what has happened to him.' So I told them, 'Whoever has any gold jewelry, take it off.' Then they gave me the gold, and I threw it into the fire, and out came this calf!'" Overall, Aaron's plea is reminiscent of "I swear, officer, I was just driving along when that tree ran out in front of my car."

Meanwhile, in the Qur'an, the main *mufsid* is outed—Samiri—and Aaron seems much more like a babysitter who has been roped to a chair as the kids went crazy.

In the Qur'an, when Moses returns from his appointment with God, he is disappointed that, in his absence, a man named Samiri has misled his people. Samiri had shaped a calf and convinced people that the calf was worthy of their worship. This was a grievous error, but Aaron had been unable to prevent people from being misled by Samiri.

It was obvious to Moses that Samiri was the culprit in this deviation from the worship of the one true God. The people said so. There was no room for doubt, and Moses could have rightfully rendered a judgment against Samiri. But he didn't. Instead of rushing to condemn Samiri, he preferred to hear him out, even in a case as clear as this one. The Qur'an narrates, "Moses said: 'What then is your case. Oh, Samiri?'"

This is the hallmark of fairness and justice, hearing out both sides and giving them an opportunity to explain their actions, even if the guilt of one side or the other seems to be established beyond doubt, as was the case of Samiri. The Qur'an advises believers to be "ever steadfast in your devotion to God, bearing witness to the truth in all equity; and never let hatred of anyone lead you into the sin of deviating from justice." Neither prejudgment nor bias, nor even enmity, should prevent a leader from rendering justice in any dispute or conflict.

The view from Islam is Moses properly delegated the leadership of the community and the management of its affairs to his teammate. In doing so, Moses defined the delegated task as follows: First, he delegated broadly but clearly by charging Aaron to act for him among his people. Second, he clarified his expectation by asking Aaron to "replace me among my people, act in the Right Way." Third, he placed appropriate limits on the delegated authority by asking Aaron not to follow the way of those who do mischief.

Thus delegation, from this perspective, is a model for defining (1) what is the task, (2) what should be the end result, and (3) what are the boundaries within which the task should be performed and results accomplished. The interaction between the one delegating (Moses) and the one to whom temporary power is delegated (Aaron), however, becomes muddied by assumptions that are often neglected in the process of delegation: As a representative of Moses, is Aaron completely responsible for everything that happens after Moses leaves?

When Moses returned to find Aaron had been unable to prevent the people from being misled by Samiri, the prophet was upset. As a servant leader, Moses stepped up at a time when other leaders would be inclined to step back and let others take the blame. Moses held Aaron accountable but assumed responsibility himself, illustrating one of the most basic rules of delegation: One can delegate authority, but ultimate responsibility still rests with the delegator. In fact, Moses prayed, "Oh, my Lord! Forgive me and my brother! Admit us to your mercy! For you are the Most Merciful of those who show mercy!"

Moses then asked for forgiveness for himself—for getting angry, and for not fulfilling his responsibility—as well as forgiveness for his brother who seemingly failed to fully exercise his authority in this delegated task, which was "replace me among my people, act in the Right Way." Significantly, Moses asked for forgiveness for himself first, which speaks to his awareness of his own role as the team leader, as the one who was ultimately responsible. As an effective leader, Moses went further and identified himself with his people and his role in this situation. After all, earlier in the Exodus, the Israelites asked Moses for an idol to which they could bow down, and no record exists of Moses' response. Perhaps that was an opportunity for a teachable moment to discuss crises of faith.

God teaches another principle in this story of delegation gone awry: One to whom a task is delegated must have the sufficient authority and resources to see it through. In the qur'anic version, when Moses was away to meet God, Samiri caused a rebellion among the people against the legitimately delegated leadership of Aaron and misled the people into deviating from the worship of God to the worship of a golden "sacred" calf. When Moses returned to his people, "he flung down the Tablet of the Law he was carrying for them. He tugged Aaron's beard and his hair, crying: 'What held you back when you saw them going astray? Why did you not fight this corruption?'" Aaron replied, "Oh, son of my mother, let go of my beard! The fold considered me weak and were about to kill me. So make not the enemies rejoice over me, nor put me among the people who are wrongdoers."

Moses' heart softened toward his brother, and he resisted judging Samiri as well, because, as the Prophet Muhammed said, "Such should be the exercise of fairness and justice even when the conclusion may seem to be obvious." However, that did not mean that there would be no punishment for the insurrection. In both the Bible and the Qur'an, the punishment was death.

At times like this, it is important to be wary of "presentism"—that is, viewing literary or historical decisions through a modern-day lens or bias. The idea that anybody should be killed for such an act of foolishness might be so repugnant to our contemporary mind-set that learning anything from it may seem impossible, but it would be intellectually dishonest to cherry-pick through a text merely to avoid unpleasantness. Besides, as unlikely as it may seem regarding executions, there is direct correlation to organizational development in this part of the Mosaic narrative as well.

In Exodus, having witnessed many of the Israelites making and then sacrificing to a graven image, God was so angry that He wanted to wipe out all of the Children of Israel and start over. "I have seen these people," the Lord said to Moses, "and they are a stiff-necked people." This description implies an unwillingness to bow their heads in respect or lift their countenances to heaven. "Now leave me alone so that my anger may burn against them and that I may destroy them," God said, "then I will make you into a great nation." But Moses pleaded with God to be patient while he tried to sort it out. "'Lord,' he said, 'why should your anger burn against your people, whom you brought out of Egypt with great power and a mighty hand?'" God relented, but Moses knew it was up to him to make it right.

Per the Qur'an, Moses gathered the elders who represented this apostasy and told them to rush toward God and beg for forgiveness, whereupon they were hit with "punishing lightning bolts and a violent quaking that stupefied their souls and bodies at once, leaving them dead." Getting hit by lightning or an earthquake as a sign of God's wrath is one of those popular media clichés, but in both the Qur'an and the Bible, there are times when it really does happen! Moses was still their leader, however, so he prayed that God would forgive the elders, and God "revived them after their death."

In Exodus, after Moses talked God out of wiping out all the refugees in anger, he stood at the camp entrance at the base of Mount Sinai and asked, "Whoever is for the Lord, come to me." As it turns out, all the men who came forward were from the Levite tribe. Then Moses explained that to make this right, "Each man strap a sword to his side. Go back and forth through the camp from one end to the other, each killing his brother and friend and neighbor." This method shows that the capital punishment that was to be carried out on the people was not conveniently directed at those the Levites did not like or had quarrels with. The Bible says about 3,000 people died that day.

With that behind him, Moses returned to the Lord on behalf of his people in hopes that this action would placate God's anger. Moses volunteered to give up his own earthly—and heavenly—life when he asked of the Lord, "Please forgive their sin—but if not, then blot me out of the book you have written." God refused, but the process of reconciliation had begun. Unlike the Qur'an, however, God does not raise anybody from the dead for a much happier ending. What is done is done. So, what could be learned from this?

It should be noted that as shocking as the number 3,000 is, it, too, has a symbolic component. The use of 1,000 in the Bible is taken to mean "immense" or "complete in quantity," and it appears hundreds of times in a non-literal capacity, not unlike our modern English phrasing,

"I would walk a thousand miles to see you again." Once more, three times 1,000 is merely an amplification implying "really, really immense" and not a real body count.

Still, stressing the legitimacy of a "really, really immense" penalty appears inconsistent with God's despair over having to drown Pharaoh's entire army just a few weeks earlier. At the very least, because the Levites were following Moses' directive that was intended to please God, the action seems unforgiving. Then again, so were the desert conditions. What modern readers may miss that original receivers of this story would have taken in stride are the narrow margins of life and death in the desert. Providing enough water, food, protection, and shelter to 600,000 people in a barren landscape that featured almost as many natural dangers as tribal enemies meant that any misstep could be catastrophic. Their safety came in numbers; disunity could be fast-acting poison.

That said, the one true meaning and intent of that particular narrative about a crisis of faith may be completely lost to scholarship. While some people of faith might relish a story of disobedience and severe punishment, if learned rabbis have been debating the inconsistencies and anomalies of the "Levites go on a killing spree" story for centuries, the casual reader should use caution in coming to any hard-and-fast conclusion of "This is what the story means." For example, some of it doesn't even make sense. Earlier in the narrative, the Bible tells us Moses had already taken the large golden calf, melted it down, smashed it into powder, mixed the granulated gold with water, and made the offending revelers drink the concoction.

Still, the sages may ask, was there a better way to handle this crisis of faith? Great leaders in times of great national crisis have to face painful decisions. Their greatness is measured by the decisions they make. A good example in recent American history is President Harry Truman's decision to drop the atomic bomb on Japan in order to end the most lethal war in history.

The founder of the State of Israel, David Ben-Gurion, is criticized to this day for two existential decisions when the future of the fledgling state hung in the balance. The first accusation is that he did not do enough to save European Jewry during the Holocaust. Unlike President Truman, Ben-Gurion did not have an atomic bomb he could drop on Berlin to end the war. His task was to use his limited resources to create the first Jewish state in the ancestral Land of Israel and do this, as he put it, "as if there is no Nazi Germany, as if there is no British occupier, and as if there is no Arab enemy."

When the modern state of Israel was born, Ben-Gurion had to make another important decision with potential long-term ramifications. His opponent, Menachem Begin, the head of his rival faction in the struggle for the state, brought an illegal armament-carrying ship from the United States, the *Altalena*, to fight a separate war to free Jerusalem. The weapons were vital for the war effort; however, Ben-Gurion knew that a sovereign state would lose international credibility if it were fighting separate wars under rival political leadership, and he ordered his men to sink the ship.

Like Moses, men like Truman and Ben-Gurion are measured among history's most impactful leaders for their willingness to bring order to chaos even through unpopular means. By rooting out those who were actively creating dysfunction and threatening a successful journey to the Promised Land, Moses ensured that the liberated Israelites became a united people who brought the knowledge of the one true God to the world. If the nation of Israel had ended at the foot of Mount Sinai in a breakdown brought on by irrational fear, distrust, and factional in-fighting, it is questionable whether there ever would have been a Bible, Christianity, a Qur'an, or Islam. As abhorrent as the deaths of "3,000" golden-calf worshipers might seem, seen from the long lens of history, the continuity of the Israelite movement appears even more pivotal.

The qur'anic version of Moses' response to the crisis of faith by some Israelites is a little easier to wrangle: lessons learned related to the corruption of worship, the punishment of the elders, and forgiveness for their transgressions. The thread that runs through this series of events is one of responsibility, opportunity to redeem oneself, the punishment that is needed to correct, and the importance of a second chance.

Looking at it from an organizational standpoint, what happens when any group deviates from its vision and mission and essentially loses its focus, if not its soul, that unique spark which distinguishes it from any other company or organization? The leader must step in and demand a wholesale turnabout, beginning with a recognition and acceptance of the grave deviation. The laws of Moses mandate honesty and fairness in business: Do not cheat by using rigged scales; do not misrepresent weights when selling produce; do not mistreat the poor; do not mistreat the stranger, "for ye were strangers in the land of Egypt." To accomplish this, the leader picks those who represent or command the rank and file and charges them to begin the turnabout by accepting their error and, if necessary, admitting it to a higher authority, which in the temporal worldly case of a business could be the sole owner, or a board of directors, or an assembly of stakeholders, or even a governmental regulating body.

Is this nothing more than a parable regarding how every manager charged with overseeing other workers should be compelled to take responsibility for their errors, especially when employees under his or her aegis are misled into wrongdoing? Whether anybody serving that manager should have known better is a separate conversation, but leaders of the rank and file must be disciplined or, in the extreme, even be punished by termination. As in the case of Moses, upper management might have to do some soul-searching, too, to determine whether it might have been sending some errant or mixed message that led to the error by Samiri or Aaron. After an internal investigation, compassion (if not forgiveness) might be in order. An opportunity for redemption can be a powerful corporate tool in a company's forward trajectory.

Finally, business realities being what they are, servant leaders also benefit from a more abstract interpretation of the Bible as well. If one reconsiders God as a market force creating downward pressure, the retribution on the idol worshipers would be akin to shutting down a failing division before it took down the whole company. No servant leader would want to see thousands of employees lose their livelihoods unless, by cutting 3,000 jobs, the leader saved 600,000 more. The goal was the

Promised Land, which was miles and years ahead, and there was a lot of ground to cover to get there.

To the extent that all great things are created in a place between method and madness, the next forty years for the Children of Israel were spent being instructed by God through God's prophet Moses as they moved through the desert until a generation of Israelites shaped by their captivity had been reconditioned or died. The biblical books of Exodus, Leviticus, Numbers, and Deuteronomy are the blueprint for the social and worship structure that has sustained Jews through periods of dislocation, suffering, and redemption. Every aspect of Hebrew life was covered through divine revelation, from clean and unclean food to the proper dimensions and measurements for just about everything. Codifying the religious rituals, sacred spaces, and purifying customs set down by God in the desert has meant that wherever Jews were persecuted and exiled, a framework existed for the practice of their faith and the maintenance of a common heritage.

The level of adherence to *halakha*—the collective Hebrew word for Judaic dietary, purity, and behavioral laws—varies among Jews from the less binding, more modernized Reform Jewish tradition to stricter Orthodox customs. Yet the foundation for all levels was laid in the Sinai desert after Moses' victory at the Red Sea and before entering the Promised Land. The overall role of ritual law in Judaism is to do God's will as originally stated in the Books of Moses, the first five books of the Bible, and interpreted by post-biblical sages. For example, a working rabbi, who would be called upon to perform many funerals, would ask the family of the deceased what kind of a person their loved one was. The typical answer would be "he or she was a good person." It may seem rather simplistic, but it illustrates that, for most Jews, ethical behavior is more important than ritual observance.

The role of ritual in Christianity varies according to denomination, but it is much more centered on worship than lifestyle choices. No official "low church–high church" paradigm list exists, but generally speaking, "low churches," such as Baptist, Pentecostal, and Quaker traditions, deemphasize sacraments and clerical authority while "high church" liturgies, such as Catholic, Orthodox, and Anglican traditions, feature a more ornate ritual worship experience with all the "smells and bells." Of course, there is some continuity in Christianity, but ritualistic expressions of faith—how and when people are baptized, communion practices, foot washing, and so on—vary so dramatically that some Christians raised in the so-called high church who attend a low-church service might feel as though they had stumbled into a gospel-singing competition or a Bible book-club meeting.

In Islam, ritual's role is also to strengthen man's relationship with God, as well as our human relationship with each other in the living world within guidelines annunciated in the Qur'an and exemplified by Muhammed. In their essence, Islamic rituals are timeless. They define and bind together the universal Muslim community even when the manner in which they are practiced differs from place to place and from time to time. Rituals of daily worship, once-in-a-lifetime pilgrimage, or annual month-long fasting all have an underlying function of bringing the practitioners socially closer within an ethos of closeness to God while still allowing for varying levels of adherence depending on the interpretation of the Qur'an and tradition.

Such are the vagaries between the faiths, over time, that a modestly dressed, head-covering, prudent-living, seventeenth-century American Puritan might feel much more at home around a modern-day American Muslim than a fashionably dressed contemporary Christian woman, but each expression traces back to Moses' successful shepherding of his gigantic human flock to the Land of Milk and Honey. All variations and branches of the Three Abrahamic faiths—from the most liberal to the most conservative—have one thing in common. God's promise to Abraham—"I will make you into a great nation, and I will bless you; I will make your name great, and you will be a blessing"—would have died in the desert dirt unless Moses succeeded at the Herculean task of bringing the Children of Israel to the land of Canaan, which God was giving to the Israelites.

It was an achievement that Moses was allowed to see but not touch. Moses and Aaron were great men, but they were not perfect. Like the generation of Israelites on whose souls Pharaoh still had his grip who the Lord knew were oppressing themselves through a lack of faith in the God that brought them out of captivity, Moses and Aaron, too, had their moments of doubt. For their own expression of faithlessness, God had told Moses and Aaron that neither would live to enjoy the Promised Land. At other times, Aaron's transgressions were seemingly more obvious; yet Moses, too, had disobeyed the Lord, and it had not gone without notice. The story concerns the waters of Meribah, also named Massah, and according to the timeline of the Exodus narrative, it was the second time—perhaps conflated with the first—that Moses asked the Lord to help him find a spring for the Israelites to drink from:

In the first month, the whole congregation of Israel entered the Wilderness of Zin and stayed in Kadesh. There Miriam died and was buried.

Now there was no water for the congregation, so they gathered against Moses and Aaron. The people quarreled with Moses and said, "If only we had perished with our brothers before the Lord! Why have you brought the Lord's assembly into this wilderness for us and our livestock to die here? Why have you led us up out of Egypt to bring us to this wretched place? It is not a place of grain, figs, vines, or pomegranates—and there is no water to drink!"

Then Moses and Aaron went from the presence of the assembly to the entrance of the Tent of Meeting. They fell facedown, and the glory of the Lord appeared to them. And the Lord said to Moses, "Take the staff and assemble the congregation. You and your brother Aaron are to speak to the rock while they watch, and it will pour out its water. You will bring out water from the rock and provide drink for the congregation and their livestock."

So Moses took the staff from the Lord's presence, just as He had commanded. Then Moses and Aaron gathered the assembly in front of the rock, and Moses said to them, "Listen now, you rebels, must we bring you water out of this rock?" Then Moses raised his hand and struck the rock twice with his staff, so that a great amount of water gushed out, and the congregation and their livestock were able to drink.

But the Lord said to Moses and Aaron, "Because you did not trust Me to show My holiness in the sight of the Israelites, you will not bring this assembly into the land that I have given them."

It was a subtle transgression, to be sure. God gave Moses a very specific instruction: Assemble the congregation, but speak to the rock. While the people are watching, the rock will become a spring. Instead, Moses brought the company of people together, making himself and Aaron sound put upon for having to quench their thirst yet again, and then he raised his hand, hit the rock twice with his staff, and never spoke to it as God had commanded.

God's admonishment highlighted how Moses had made himself seem as if he had the power to perform miracles on his own, if only for a moment. As a result, Aaron would pass on the first day of the fifth month on the top of Mount Hor, and he was mourned for thirty days.

Forty years later, his eyes undimmed and his body just as vigorous as it had always been, Moses climbed Mount Nebo at the edge of the land of Canaan, where he could see "Gilead as far as Dan, all of Naphtali, the land of Ephraim and Manasseh, all the land of Judah as far as the Western Sea, the Negev, and the region from the Valley of Jericho [the City of Palms] all the way to Zoar." This was the land that God had promised to Abraham, Isaac, and later Israel.

The Bible does not speak of a self-sacrificial death for Moses, and neither does the Qur'an. The concept of personal responsibility is deeply ingrained in Islamic theology. In the qur'anic view, "whatever [wrong] any human being commits rests upon himself alone; and no bearer of burdens shall be made to bear another's burden." From an Islamic perspective, God sends guidance for mankind through divine messengers and prophets who proclaim that guidance and practice it among their populace. The people will either accept that guidance or reject it of their own free will, and they are rewarded or punished accordingly on the

Day of Judgement. Unlike in Christian theology, nobody else can bear another person's sins.

Moses had done his job. God was calling him home. Moses, the servant of the Lord, and the servant leader of the Children of Israel, died in the land of Moab, where the Israelites grieved for thirty days, "until the time of weeping and mourning for Moses came to an end." He was 120 years old but still in his prime.

The Qur'an does not give an age, but the Muslim tradition does add an interesting story the Bible does not: This was not the first time that Moses faced death. At some point earlier, there is this account in the Hadith:

> The Angel of Death was sent to Moses. When he arrived Moses punched him in the eye. The Angel returned to his Lord and said, "You have sent me to a slave who does not want to die." God said, "Return to him and tell him to put his hand on the back of an ox and for every hair that will come under it, he will be granted one year of life." Moses said, "Oh, Lord! What will happen after that?" God replied, "then death." Moses said, "Let it come now!" Moses then requested God to let him die close to the Holy Land so that he would be at a distance of a stone's throw from it.

And so he was. There was no grave, no marker. Some scholars say that, at the last moment, just this close to their new home, some of the Israelites might have made a shrine of it and worshiped Moses instead of God and nullified the efforts of this most humble man. Others suggest there could be no burial because there was no body. Moses had ascended into heaven on top of Mount Nebo, but there is no record of that, either.

What we do know regarding Moses' death is the record of his most significant achievement as a servant leader. This act could only have come after his death; yet it arguably speaks louder about the character of this humble shepherd than the Exodus, the parting of the Red Sea, and the Ten Commandments because all of those were possible only because of God. All leaders are responsible for their teams, but many fall victim to their own egos by believing that they are irreplaceable, that "I alone can fix it," or cleave to the fallacy of thinking of themselves as the only one who can do a job right, so why bother trying to find a successor?

Moses understood that his growth depended on helping others grow. Greater than Moses' equanimity, his persistence, his patience, his willingness to delegate, his eagerness to take feedback and be given advice, and his insistence on assuming blame and sharing credit was this last great act of servant leadership: Moses had trained his replacement. Moses' successor, Joshua, son of Nun, had been his assistant since the beginning of the Exodus; he was with Moses when he received the Ten Commandments, and he also later served as a militia leader and a spy who risked his life to prepare Moses for the challenges ahead. So, after thirty days of mourning,

> Joshua son of Nun was filled with the spirit of wisdom because Moses had laid his hands on him. So the Israelites obeyed him and did as the LORD had commanded Moses. Since that time, no prophet has arisen in Israel like Moses, whom the LORD knew face to face, who did all the signs and wonders that the LORD sent him to do against the land of Egypt—to Pharaoh and all his officials and all his land—by all the mighty acts of power and awesome deeds that Moses performed in the sight of all Israel.

THE MOSAIC OF CHAPTER 6

1. Which phase of Moses' life can you relate to most?
2. Which characteristic of Moses' leadership do you think is most important?
3. Does the death of 3,000 Israelites at the hands of the Levites have to be justified? If so, how?
4. The future of all three Abrahamic religions hinged on how Moses acted after descending with the Ten Commandments.
5. Moses and Aaron were both prevented from experiencing the fruits of their labors, but were the reasons just?
6. Great leaders are defined by how well they train their successors.

Conclusion

On Reaching the Promised Land— Together

Good leadership is critical to the success of any group. Good leadership draws its inspiration from life stories of great men and women, many of whom (such as Moses) set examples of conduct and character guided by God. Such are the prophets and messengers of God, sent to humankind with divine revelation that leads ordinary men and women to extraordinary success in extraordinary times such as these.

Whenever political leaders appear particularly untrustworthy, it is up to all of us to offer an alternative example for others to witness. Being trustworthy does not require a world stage. Trustworthiness includes a broad spectrum of qualities that employers seek, including honesty, loyalty, and truthfulness. Often trustworthiness may be the most desirable characteristic because while competence and skills might be acquired through learning and training, honesty and truthfulness are a part of one's character that has been baked in and is never fleeting.

The story of Moses in all the phases of his life, even in this brief discourse, offers Jews, Christians, and Muslims valuable lessons in purposeful, trustworthy leadership and the art of working together, especially in times of tyrants. In these lessons, people of all faiths—and even none at all—discover the ancient and time-tested origins of present-day leadership, organizational behavior, and interpersonal communication concepts as they were played out millennia ago, before, during, and after the reception of the Ten Commandments.

Leadership is a multifaceted phenomenon knit together from a set of complex behaviors, a phenomenon that is historical in its roots and ageless in the wisdom from which it springs. Recognizing the history-changing success of Moses' efforts against incredible odds and how any of us can incorporate his best practices into all our endeavors will enhance our ability to perform well and achieve satisfaction, God willing.

For God worshipers whose belief system is rooted in divine scripture, understanding leadership lessons from the life of Moses will only deepen their understanding of the role of faith in personal and organizational relationships. People of faith are better able to internalize contemporary theories and models when they can relate them to their spiritual and moral underpinnings.

The historical circumstances of the Moses story are different from the complexity of this modern life, but closer examination has shown that, perhaps with regard to overcoming a tyrant who stood in the way of progress and success, it was not so much. In contemporary organizations—from the simplicity of a family, a neighborhood, or a company to an entire nation-state—new modes of thinking and relating to each other have led to exciting breakthroughs; yet, at the core, human instincts and behavior, ingenuity, and initiative, and the struggle to discover the right course of action, all remain rooted in the same immutable nature of every person who has ever existed. Divinely inspired guidance is at once ancient, modern, and contemporary.

For example, God knew that sometimes the right way to deal with a harsh and unrepentant deceiver is not in a like manner but in quite the opposite way. God sought a humble servant leader to overcome a ruthless overbearing tyrant because communication is getting a message across, not getting even. God needed a messenger with two major characteristics: competence and trustworthiness. These qualities were always apparent in Moses. Jethro, the elderly Midianite priest whose daughters

Moses helped at the desert well, recognized Moses' true character the first time the would-be prophet was hired to be a shepherd.

Next, Moses took an inventory of the skills required for the job as God described it, assessed his own abilities, and recognized his limitations. It is critical for the success of any mission for leaders to understand what skills are needed and to identify one's own strengths and weaknesses in the context of what is required. Confident leaders do not shy away from confronting their own limitations. Any work should be judged not just by how well it was done but also by how much it benefited those it affected.

In his case, Moses recognized that his communication skills were not as effective as they should be. Moses asked God to remove the difficulty he had in public speaking. In stating his requests to God, Moses revealed his pragmatic approach and his ability to assess potential problems. He showed an awareness of his own limitations, a level of emotional intelligence that is an exemplary quality for a good leader. Moses did not ask to have his speech impediment removed so that he could orate impressively. Instead, he asked God to remove the hitch in his communication so that those who listened to him could understand him better and not be confused or distracted. This is the core of communication: the receiver of the message should understand the message as it was intended. Communication is complete not when the sender sends the message, but rather when the receiver receives it and ascribes meaning to it.

With his difficulties and limitations in mind, Moses proposed a solution: Form a team with his brother Aaron to fulfill the mission, with each teammate complementing the leader's skills. Having granted that request, God presents the brothers as one unit. For the team to be effective, Moses expected Aaron to participate in sharing the load and not be a mere bystander. The plural subjects in the scriptures such as "*They said*" and "*We fear*" indicate a process of active consultation between the two of them. The leader's job is to determine which teammate is suited to play which part and when. As the task grew larger in the desert, Moses added more team members at the suggestion of Jethro.

Leadership produces unpredictable dynamics involving the leader's personality traits and the collective behavior of people being led. Foremost in these personal characteristics are the abilities to communicate, to function as a team, and to delegate. Adding strength is not only having more energy to do something but also taking advantage of the synergy in doing it. Synergy makes the work of two halves better than that of one whole (persons or processes or resources).

The life of Moses offers other moral, spiritual, and practical guidance to aspiring and proven leaders and managers. Scriptural texts are best studied seeking answers to questions because their fundamental purpose is to guide the seeker. Leaders and managers will be well advised to study the life of Moses with such questions in mind as they may relate to their own experiences and challenges. Jews, Christians, and Muslims will not be disappointed in the wisdom and insight they gain toward fulfillment and success in their personal and professional lives when they look at a situation through the Moses lens.

The relationship between two Arabic words might be informative in this case. The Arabic word for "praise" is transliterated into English as *tasbih*. *Tasbih* is connected often to the Arabic word for "remembrance" (*zikr*) in the context of accomplishing an important objective such as community building. The mission to which Moses and Aaron were directed was the release of the Israelites from the clutches of Pharaoh. To them, the mission encompassed the *tasbih* and the *zikr* of God because when God's will was manifested, the people also earned God's praise and remembrance.

Praising and remembering God—keeping our faith life central to our goals—crystallizes our mission and keeps all people of faith moving forward in our battles with Pharaoh. Of course, the pharaoh that stands between us and freedom today is not one man but many men and women in positions of power who manipulate social, financial, and political systems selfishly to their advantage regardless of the impact on others. Their name is legion, for they are many.

Accomplishing this book also took a lot of *tasbih* and *zikr* on the part of the authors. First, the very act of writing this required thousands of hours of dedication and coordination between three busy people of faith who all praise God differently. Second, remembrance was strained because, well, all three of the authors are getting older, and it's hard to remember anything these days.

Yet, as a team—one Jew, one Christian, and one Muslim—speaking together in one voice, working together toward a common goal of building on what binds instead of being enslaved by those who seek to divide, we present this book to the new generation of would-be leaders who must fight tyranny whenever it exists until the day the prophecy is fulfilled: "Nation shall not raise a sword against another nation, nor shall they learn war anymore."

Index

CPSIA information can be obtained
at www.ICGtesting.com
Printed in the USA
BVHW030200110121
597530BV00005B/24